# *I* am a *Woman*

## *Healing the*
## *Feminine Spirit*

## Yvonne Martinez

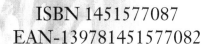

ISBN 1451577087
EAN-139781451577082

Distributed by

## www.StillwaterLavender.com

**Printed in United States of America**

> ## *Dedicated to the most important women in my lifetime ~*

My grandmother, Nola Rebecca Canady

My mother, Nola LaVerne Battinich

My sister, Pamela Joyce Cooley

My daughter, Noel Yvonne Martinez

and

My mother-in-love, Gavina Martinez

My spiritual mom, Wanda Rogers

My close friend, Laurie Ostrem

My close friend, Pauline Hailstone

and

In memory of my dearest friend, Lydia McChesney


**We have laughed together, cried together, prayed for each other, loved each other, and stood by one another in tough times as well as good.**


*I thank God for your influence in my life.*

## Recommendations

With Yvonne being part of my Pastoral Counseling team, I have first hand experience with her insight, passion and vision in helping women become whole and healed.

For women who struggle with issues identity, femininity and sexuality, *"I am a Woman - Healing the Feminine Spirit"*, dares to dive into deep waters of healing and deliverance and bring to the surface a path for freedom.

Written from a place of depth and clarity, compassion and healing, Yvonne Martinez' bold new book hits the mark in ministering to the underlying and unresolved issues that many women face. Perhaps, more importantly, she has resourced the church with a vital tool to help those who minister to women in areas of brokenness.

*Dawna DeSilva*
*Founder, Bethel Sozo, International*
*Director, Transformation Center*
*Bethel Church*
*Redding, CA*

Yvonne Martinez' latest book, "*I Am a Woman - Healing the Feminine Spirit*" is the fruit of over 25 years of ministry to women, drawing on God's grace and wisdom to heal and free His beloved daughters.

Walking through her own journey, Yvonne understands many of the barriers and mindsets that have kept women in bondage. She has given women a path to freedom; loving her "sisters" enough to share her insights and wisdom.

Written with honesty and clarity, this is a book that will encourage and empower all who read it.

*Dr. Katherine Weyrens, Psychiatrist*
*Grace Connections Mental Health*
*Topeka, Kansas*

# Table of Contents

# I am a Woman

*I am a Woman*

made in GOD'S image

**accepted   adopted**

**redeemed**

*enlightened  endowed  blessed*

**set free   set apart   loved**

*holy  healed  delivered*

*refined   renewed   equipped*

covered   complete   blameless

**unashamed   unafraid**

**forgiven**

*H*is chosen

*H*is friend

*H*is bride

*I am a Woman*

made in GOD'S image

*destined for such a time as this ~*

I Am A Woman© ~ Yvonne Martinez~ 2005

## *I* am a *Woman*
### Scripture references

Gen. 1:27, Acts 15:8, Eph. 1:5, Eph. 1:7
Eph. 1:18, Eph. 1:6, Eph. 1:3
Jn. 8:36, Ps. 4:3, Jn. 3:16, Eph. 1:4
Is. 53:5, Col. 1:13, Is. 48:10
Ps. 103:5, Heb. 13:21, Ez. 16:8
Jn. 15:11, Eph. 1:4, Ps. 34:5, 1Jn. 4:18
Col. 1:14, Jn. 15:16, Jn. 15:15
Rev. 21.9, Gen. 1:27, Est. 4:14

# 1

## *Introduction*

*"The Spirit of the Sovereign Lord is on me, because the Lord has anointed me to preach good news to the poor. He has sent me to bind up the brokenhearted, to proclaim freedom for the captives and release from darkness for the prisoners..."*
—*Isaiah 61:1*

It is the quality and character of being female that makes us women. So, for the purpose of this book, the feminine spirit is that place in a woman which uniquely defines her identity, intimacy, femininity and sexuality.

A woman's feminine spirit is crushed or broken not only through loss, trauma, or abuse but from what she does to herself through choices and reaction to what has happened to her. To protect herself, a woman may draw upon protective barriers and spiritual strongholds that lead to mistaken identity, misplaced loyalty, distorted intimacy, compromised femininity, and perverted sexuality.

*I am a Woman* is presented from a candid and graphic perspective with terminology and content that might make some of your hair curl! I recommend reading my book, *Dancing on the Graves of Your Past*, for a better understanding and backdrop to the healing process for loss, trauma and abuse.

While not all women will relate personally to every aspect of the issues I present in *I am a Woman*, they should find greater insight and help for women who are stuck in self-destructive patterns. Ultimately, those of you who spend ministry hours with women will find insight and prophetic direction to help them discover their greatest destiny.

Processing through the content of *I am a Woman ~ Healing the Feminine Spirit* with ministry and healing prayer is available through my workshops and a forthcoming DVD series.

I write from 25 years of women's ministry, prophetic counseling, inner healing and deliverance, as well as through my own personal journey of healing.

In this season, I am unwilling to continue to ignore the conflicts affecting and afflicting so many women who struggle with identity, intimacy, femininity and sexuality. I am unwilling to sweep under the rug the battle for freedom that has undermined and trapped women in roles of performance with religious constraints.

My purpose isn't to blame or find fault with historical oppression against women, their generations, families or abusers. Nor is it to find fault with the church or men. It is also not to condone or excuse a woman's attitude, behavior and wrong choices.

I open up a panoramic view of struggles, painful core issues, mindsets, strongholds, as well as choices and patterns women have followed to soothe their pain and mask their brokenness.

Frankly, ladies, this means we are going to get down and dirty, take off the bandages and look at the mess.

Eve, the first woman and mother, represents the fundamental identity given toward women, their gender role and authority. Through Eve's words and actions, it is felt that the true nature of women is revealed; her story tells men (and women) what women are really like.

From a biased position against Eve, she represents a prevalent belief that women are by nature disobedient, beguiled, weak-willed, prone to temptation and evil, disloyal, untrustworthy, deceitful, seductive, and motivated in their thoughts and behavior purely by self-interest. Who then can trust her when she can't trust herself?

Eve did make a mistake, a bad choice, and sinned against God's command. However, so did Adam. When God sent Jesus to restore us to Him, men and women both were redeemed. When men and women receive Jesus as forgiveness for mistakes, bad choices, and sin, they (men and women) are fully pardoned, redeemed, delivered and healed through Jesus' death and resurrection. Jesus set women free from all curses and empowered her to thrive and succeed, not in the image of a man, but as a woman created in the image of God.

The belief in women as a prototype of unredeemed Eve is not part of God's plan. The truth is that she is valued and desperately needed to release the Glory of God through the compassion, caring, nurturing and merciful mother's heart of God to other women and the world.

Just like a natural family flourishes with both dad and mom to bring balance, love and leadership to the home and children, so the family of God needs both a father and mother image to bring love and leadership into His Kingdom and His children.

Religion doesn't know what to do with women, not to mention hurting or broken women, and especially not strong, powerful women. In many cases, tradition, steeped in patriarchal leadership, has adopted both spoken and unspoken rules of what is acceptable for woman.

In a nut shell (if it is at all possible to fit anything into a nut shell), we'll take a look at the places of brokenness and healing to the delicate areas of:

Girl – Identity

Daughter – Inheritance

Wife – Intimacy

Mother – Authority

*I am a Woman* will offer healing solutions to satisfy the deep longing and hunger for genuine intimacy, femininity and sexuality. *I am a Woman ~ Healing the Feminine Spirit* workshops offer deeper personal ministry through inner healing prayer, bringing freedom and healing to the feminine spirit.

*I am a Woman* joins a parade of women, shoulder to shoulder in leadership, serving to help women embrace their future. I am proud to be a woman in this most epic supernatural season for women in church history.

Thank you, Papa God, for making it possible! Come on girls, let's hold hands and jump in together!

# 2

## Trouble Right Here

*"For the brokenness of the daughter of my people*
*I am broken; I mourn, dismay has taken hold of me.*
*Is there no balm in Gilead? Is there no physician there?*
*Why then has not the health of the daughter of*
*my people been restored?"*
*—Jeremiah 8:21,22 NASB*

If I didn't think I'd get hit by lightning, I'd like to remove Proverbs 31 from my bible. Now it isn't that I don't love God's Word. I do. There's just something about the perfection of Ms. P-31 that puts pressure on me. Maybe without TV, CD, DVD, Blue Ray, cell phones, Yahoo, Facebook, My Space, Twitter, computer login codes, security codes, passwords, calendars and grocery lists, I'd be able to make the grade! Read Proverbs 31, then fast forward to year 2011.

Ms. P-31 puts on her superwoman cape and faster than a bullet heads for ballet lessons, music lessons, sports games, doctors and dentists, conferences with the teacher, PTA committee, and ladies prayer team.

More powerful than a locomotive, she manages family, home, ministry, businesses, corporations, and the complexity of today's menstrual pad selection of wings, no wings, overnights, maxi, mini, panti liner or shields, heavy, slender, petite, regular, short, long, or extra long.

Able to leap tall buildings in a single bound, she produces healthy meals, keeps all the whites separated from darks, eradicates dust, maintains white teeth, dry arm pits, and with peak discernment navigates through the breakfast cereal at the grocery store. She prays without ceasing, serves in the nursery, classroom or prayer circle, always available to a hurting friend, exercises daily and has energy for a spontaneous robust roll in the hay with her husband while warding off the 7 demons of menopause: itchy, bitchy, sweaty, sleepy, bloated, forgetful, and dried up!

Now that's pressure!

On the other side of the P-31 picture, women have given up and betrayed the very essence of who they were destined to be. Many women are stressed and

18

depressed, covering their pain with disordered eating, prescription drugs, too many glasses of wine, fantasy and/or sexual indulgences, anger and rebellion.

Women are hurting and they are in our churches as well as in our communities.

> *"I used prescription medication, anti-depressants and sleeping pills for almost 10 years and finally asked for help from my Christian friends.*
> *I felt worse after they stopped returning my calls."*
> **Marie**

Marie wanted to stop the addictive cycle of pre-scription drugs she had relied on for almost 10 years af-ter her husband died. She reached out to her church for help but felt rejected and judged. Instead of coming alongside Marie, her women's ministry leader took her name off the member's roster "until she felt better."

There is both a tidal wave and an undercurrent of enormous proportion and women are on the front lines in a battle for their life.

In case you haven't noticed, *"we have trouble, my friend, right here in River City,"* as suggested in the lyrics echoed by Professor Harold Hill in the musical production, *Music Man*.

Crises in the feminine spirit are unveiled as we look at the increase of childhood sexual abuse, single moms, multiple failed marriages, the rise in female auto-immune disease, heart disease, breast and female gynecological cancers, sexually transmitted diseases, female sexual addictions, and the overall decrease in morals and significant increase in search for a spiritual connection.

> **"I just turned 59 and this is the first time I ever told anyone I had two abortions." Ann**

When Ann became pregnant at 16, her parents took her on vacation to another state for an abortion. She wasn't given a choice. Just before college graduation Ann became pregnant again. This time she willingly went to a local clinic for an abortion. Ann's story of terminating pregnancies chronicles the lives of many women in the church who live in the silence of post abortion shame.

Statistics are typically boring, but these are not simply numbers. These are truths that affect "our people" that is, our daughters, sisters, mothers, and us.

They reflect sources of deep wounding and bring to the forefront tangible evidence of the crises in the feminine spirit.

❖ 1 in 4 girls is molested before the age of 18 and more than 20% before the age of 8.

❖ 39 million survivors of childhood sexual abuse exist in America today.

❖ Girls who are sexually abused are 3 times more likely to develop psychiatric disorders.

❖ 52% of female teens are sexually active.

❖ 26% of girls age 15 have had intercourse.

❖ By their late teens, 3 of 4 girls have had intercourse and 2 of 3 had more than 2 partners.

❖ 6 in 10 pregnancies occur between ages 18-19.

❖ 2 in 10 girls will be pregnant at least once before 20 years of age.

❖ 60% of teen pregnancies are preceded by molestation.

❖ 19 million new sexually-transmitted infections occur each year, almost half of them among age 15 to 24.

❖ 1 in 3 girls contract a STD by age 24.

❖ 1 in 5 rapes against women are by intimate partners. Only one-half of rapes are ever reported to police.

❖ Children witness 36% of domestic violence assaults.

- ❖ 25% of women have been raped or physically assaulted by a spouse, former spouse, current partner, or on a date.

- ❖ 34% of women are victims of sexual coercion.

- ❖ 70% of homicide victims are female. 64% were killed by people they knew.

- ❖ Approx. 1,700,000 women are stalked annually and 76% of them were killed by their stalker.

- ❖ 80% of the 600,000 to 800,000 victims trafficked across international borders are women. Women are violated through prostitution, sexual exploitation, labor, slavery, and organ removal.

- ❖ 50% of women in prison were abused as children.

- ❖ 50% of first marriages fail.

- ❖ 20% of married women have been unfaithful.

- ❖ 68% would have an affair if they believed they wouldn't get caught.

- ❖ 72% of women with children over 1 year of age are working outside the home.

- ❖ 1 in 5 women struggle with eating disorders or disordered eating.

- ❖ In a study of girls, age 8 to 10, 50% were unhappy with their size.

- ❖ 28% of those who admit to sexual addiction are women.

- ❖ 1 in 6 women struggle with pornography.

- ❖ 47% of families say pornography is a problem in their home.

❖ 7.5% women admit they have same-sex desire.

❖ 35 million women have some sort of auto-immune disease.

❖ Plastic surgery is the most requested gift by girls graduating high school.

❖ Women received 92% of the 9.3 million plastic surgeries performed, and each year terminated 1.3 million pregnancies by abortion.

❖ 30,000 – 40,000 women each year successfully transgender to male.

❖ Of the estimated living Americans, more females attempt suicide than males at a ratio of 3 women for each man.

❖ Women who were molested as children are 8 times more likely to get cancer.

❖ Top 6 female-related deaths are from:

  o Heart disease

  o Breast cancer

  o Stroke

  o Chronic obstructive pulmonary disease (COPD)

  o Alzheimer's

  o Diabetes

Over two decades ago, a survey of men at a Promise Keepers event revealed over 50% in attendance were involved with pornography within one week of attending the event. At events like this across the USA, Christian men boldly confessed and repented for their failure of keeping promises to God, their wives and their families.

Women have been told for years to submit and remain loyal in the face of betrayal and abuse. Finally, within the context of men's confessions of unfaithfulness and addictions, the admissions gave liberation, validation, and voice to Christian women suffering in the backdraft. Men's mistakes finally echoed the pain that had previously been so easily dismissed and unattended; women have been sexualized, victimized, abused, neglected and abandoned.

Women not only *feel* shame, they believe it is who they are. That is, at the very core of their womanhood there is something bad or something is deeply wrong.

Women confide in me, confessing their greatest fears and disclosing their deepest secrets. I watch them attempt to negotiate a place of peace amidst a conflict of truths. They wrestle for a delicate balance, a compromise, between who they feel they are and who they want to be.

Women have accepted religious protocol and performance because it made them look presentable, shrink-fitting into a package that is too tight, too restrictive and downright uncomfortable. They become what is acceptable, wearing the masks, working hard to make up for mistakes, silently wondering if this is as good as it gets. They are like beautiful birds in a cage waiting for freedom to fly and experience the joy and benefits Jesus died to give them.

Names and faces are invisible unless you take time to look into their eyes, see their hearts, and listen to them. I see them and if you look you'll see them, too.

They are multi-cultural and multi-generational; women and daughters from broken families who never had the opportunity to be little girls, seen and loved, nurtured and adored. No matter the age, they're handicapped by tradition, culture or a previous genera-tion's lack, fighting a battle to obtain what they missed as young girls.

With much of the Christian church in revival, announcing testimonies of healing and miracles, so many women have never left the prison cell of shame, fear, or judgment. Shackles of depression, desperation, pride, idolatry or rebellion have kept them bound to choices that contribute to the overall mess in their life.

As you continue through *I am a Woman*, you will discover the greater truth about yourself as a woman and about the God who loves you.

The door to freedom is unlocked! Jesus didn't die on the Cross and resurrect from the grave so we would be handicapped and "survive." We are saved, healed, and set-free; overcomers called and empowered by God to bring His Kingdom to earth.

There is a way through the prison door into real freedom. Those of us who have made it through are reaching in to help our sisters still on the journey...she may be an unsaved woman or perhaps, the woman who sits next to us in church.

God partnered with us when He gave us Jesus who died on the Cross and shed His Blood. Jesus took our sins (shame, blame, sickness and yes, mistakes) and spiritual death upon Himself and through a Divine exchange gave us complete amnesty and freedom. Then, Jesus rose from the dead and returned to His Father in Heaven creating a bridge of reconciliation uniting Heaven and earth. He did it so we could be free (Galatians 5:1).

However, the purpose is more than freedom, although freedom is good! I believe the greater revelation for us in this epic season of supernatural activity in the church is to prophetically discern and heal the barriers within our own gender.

Presenting conditions and manifested symptoms reflect insight into the distortion of a woman's true identity. We can take the barriers and strongholds and use them as a mirror to reflect the high calling to which women are commissioned.

Women who are truly free embrace their Godly identity, inheritance, intimacy and authority. I believe we are the generation of women who rise up in Kingdom partnership, seated in Heavenly places with Christ Jesus (Ephesians 2:6.)

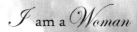

It is time for women to take their most honored position of authority; releasing the mother's heart of God to the next generation.

## Statistical Resources

- Data from the Bureau of Justice Statistics' National Crime Victimization Survey (NCVS) and the Federal Bureau of Investigation's (FBI) Uniform Crime Reporting Program's (UCR) Supplementary Homicide Reports (SHR). Female Victims of Violence September 30, 2009. Provides the current findings on nonfatal and fatal violent crimes committed against females. http://now.org/issues/violence/stats.html

- American Bar Association, Survey of Recent Statistics, Commission on Domestic Violence. http://new.abanet.org/domesticviolence/Pages/Statistics

- Divorce Rate http://www.divorcerate.org

- Students Against Destructive Decisions http://www.sadd.org

- Walsh, SJ, LM. Autoimmune Diseases: A Leading Cause of Death among Young and Middle-Aged Women in the United States. American Journal of Public Health. 2000;90:1463-1465

- Center for Disease Control and Prevention http://www.cdc.gov/cancer

- Women Issues - Top 10 Leading Causes of Female Deaths http://ezinearticles.com

- Driver, E. (1989). Introduction. *Child Sexual Abuse: A Feminist Reader*, 1-68

- Darkness to Light Organization – Confronting Child Sexual Abuse with Courage http://www.darkness2light.org/KnowAbout/statistics

- Transsexual Women's Studies Successes http://ai.eecs.umich.edu/people/conway/TSsucceses/ TSsuccesses.html

- Plastic Surgery Research Info http://www.cosmeticplasticsurgerystatis-tics.com/statistics.html#2008-FACTS

- Abortion Statistics http://www.abortiontv.com/Misc/AbortionStatistics.

- Kinsey Institute Research in Sex, Gender & Re-production. http://www.kinseyinstitute.org/resources/FAQ.html#homosexuality

- The National Institute of Mental Health - Eating Disorders  http://www.nimh.nih.gov

- Statistics on Working Moms http://workforcemoms.org/statistics-on-working-moms

- Suicide. Prevention, Awareness and Support http://www.suicide.org/suicide-statistics.html

- Safe Families http://www.safefamilies.org/sfStats.php

- 28% those admitting to sexual addiction are women (internet-filter-review.com)

- 34% of female readers of Today's Christian Woman's online newsletter admitted to intentionally accessing Internet porn in a recent poll and 1 out of every 6 women, including Christians, struggles with an addiction to pornography (Today's Christian Woman, Fall 2003).

# 3

## Who's Your Mama?

*"...As is the mother, so is her daughter."*
*—Ezekiel 16:44 (KJV)*

The greatest human tragedy is the absence and loss of knowing Jesus. The greatest female tragedy is the absence and loss of a mother.

Psychological, social, and spiritual climates in the home define our identity as daughters. The struggle for female identity and significance is increased without loving and present parents to nurture and pattern the stages of growth from the role of daughter to wife and mother.

The loss of either parent can leave daughters feeling lonely, incomplete, and depressed. However, for many daughters the loss of a mother feels like a loss of herself. A daughter will grieve the loss of her mother whether it is due to death, abandonment, or from living with an emotionally or physically absent and unavailable mother.

If there is a break or discrepancy between our relationship with our mother and who God says we are, we will wrestle to reconcile becoming who God intended while battling the absence or strongholds of our mothers and former female generations.

> *"Mom was never happy and finally left when I was 15. I've always thought it was because of me. What was the matter with me anyway?" Sarah*

Carrying the identity of an unhealed past, Sarah worked hard to bear up under extreme pressures. Even after she married, she faced increasing responsibility coupled with economic hardships, sickness and stress, often patterning her decisions and choices in the footsteps of her unhappy mother.

> *"I think she knew it was happening (pause) ...*
> *she must have known (pause)...*
> *but when I tried to tell her,*
> *she yelled and called me a liar." Morgan*

Yes, Morgan's dad was absent, abusive and demanding, but anger raged against her mom who turned her head and denied the abuse, not standing up to protect herself or Morgan.

Daughters who watched their mothers endure abuse were angry at mom for not protecting herself. Additionally, a daughter may contend with an angry, cold mom and the absence of a loving, nurturing connection.

If the mother views herself as a victim of circumstances, or is a victim of her husband, the daughter may feel sorry for her and fear losing her. This dynamic makes it very hard for the daughter to see her mother as an abuser. The truth is that people can be both - victims in one context, and abusers in another.

The more a daughter identifies with her mother, the harder it is to separate her identity from her abuser; a crucial step in healing. If mom did stand up and fight, separating or divorcing in protection of the daughter, mom was strapped with her own betrayal.

Often the daughter blamed herself for breaking up the home resulting in mom's emotional and economic hardships.

Boy, (or should I say "girl") this got close to home for me! When women began to tell me about their mother issues, I felt increasingly uncomfortable, internal fireworks exploded and rockets launched, triggering my own mother-daughter stuff.

I carry an awesome testimony of healing from the abuses of my father and men. However, in one quick flash, I recognized my whole life had been protecting my mom, and yet never experiencing a deep connection from her until very late in her life.

My mom endured beating, broken bones, and bruises from my dad, and much of the abuse I witnessed. Mom remarried, divorced, and remarried again. Her haunting past chasing at her heels, she attempted suicide, taking too many sleeping pills washed down with a steady stream of alcohol.

At her lowest, she bravely checked herself into a drug and alcohol program, reunited her heart with Jesus and stopped drinking. Her focus shifted toward her own recovery, staying sober, finishing her GED, and volunteering at church.

Her behavior and lifestyle changed for the good but she was still distanced from me. The words that stung the deepest were the words she never spoke. Issues with my mom were filled with denial, co-dependency, love and hate. All growing up, I vowed I'd **never** be like my mom. But, in fact, the truth was I had followed in her footsteps of abusive and broken relationships, shame, and low self esteem.

When I gave my heart to Jesus and the destructive patterns stopped, I was pressed into what I call "double work." That is, learning to do what was right while trying to clean up the mess and unfortunately it didn't happen overnight!

As my mom and I grew older, I was able to let go and forgive, giving myself permission to be free, no longer needing her approval and acceptance. It was a painful process of unraveling myself, as well as my loyalty and identity from her brokenness.

My own healing journey made it possible for me to build a genuine relationship with my mom and before she passed away, my heart had completely changed toward her. As I let go of expectations and looked at life through her eyes, I felt more compassion and love for her, realizing she never received the freedom she tried to find at church.

Often I could pray with her and our relationship changed. I came to believe I really was important to her. In the last years I was there for her, of course, but now it was because of a healthy love.

As you may know, emotionally needy women are skilled in setting up others to fill their unmet emotional needs. If a mom didn't feel loved, safe, secure, protected, valued and accepted before she had children, she may use her daughter in an attempt to fulfill her unmet needs.

When tension builds and nowhere to turn, often the pain in emotionally needy mothers turns to her daughter. Moms may even reject their daughters in an attempt to self-protect.

> **"She never said anything when I told her I started my period but she was mad and tossed a package of sanitary pads at me." Susan**

When Susan entered puberty, with her breasts growing and starting her menstrual cycle, Susan's mom was angry and emotionally withdrew. Susan's mom later confessed it was at puberty her own sexual abuse began. Mom's reaction was her way of protecting herself when her own sexual abuse issues were triggered.

A mother with an unmet need for respect might try to demand that her daughter "respect" her. To fill her unmet need to feel loved, she might try to manipulate the daughter into performing what she perceives as acts of love. Mom, in order to fill her unmet need to feel appreciated, might try to spoil her daughter and then constantly remind the daughter of all the things she does for her and all the sacrifices she makes for her.

## Characteristics of emotionally abusive mothers~

- ❖ Shifting responsibility for mom's feelings or happiness
- ❖ Threatening rejection or abandonment
- ❖ Threatening with vague, unstated consequences
- ❖ Using force
- ❖ Invalidating daughter's feelings
- ❖ Placing undeserved guilt
- ❖ Placing undeserved blame
- ❖ Dominating conversations
- ❖ Refusing to apologize
- ❖ Always needing to have the last word
- ❖ Judging or rejecting daughter's friends
- ❖ Locking daughter out of the house
- ❖ Using punishments and rewards to manipulate and control
- ❖ Invading daughter's privacy
- ❖ Under-estimating
- ❖ Failing to show trust in daughter or her decisions
- ❖ Labeling
- ❖ Criticizing
- ❖ Judging
- ❖ Giving the silent treatment
- ❖ Withdrawing affection as punishment
- ❖ Failing to give real explanations
- ❖ Giving non-explanations such as "because it is wrong" or "because I said so" or "because it is a sin"

Mom's message, whether spoken or implied is, "if you don't fill my needs, I will reject or abandon you." Daughter eventually learns it is impossible to make mother happy. No matter what she does, it is never enough, causing her to feel like a failure in her own ability to nurture and comfort. A daughter in this situation feels inadequate and overwhelmed, facing an impossible burden yet still trying her best to do the impossible.

By the time she is a teen, a daughter can feel drained and empty, insecure and afraid of failure, disapproved, rejected and abandoned.

---

*"I don't understand why she hated me so much. Even when I tried to stay out of her way, she would get mad at me. One time I was just sitting outside and she burst through the door and started kicking me in the back. She was angry because I hadn't folded the laundry the right way.*
*I was about 6 years old." Nancy*

---

Growing up, Nancy told me she never talked back to her mom, always walked on egg shells, trying to be a good girl and not upset her mom. Despite a lifetime of effort, Nancy's mom has never showed affection or approval.

A daughter may deny or ignore mom's abuse, discounting and minimizing her own needs. She can't afford, emotionally, to risk being rejected by her mother.

> *"When Dad lost his job Mom went to work.*
> *When she came home she was angry and demanding*
> *I help more in the house.*
> *I wanted my mom to be happy so I tried harder.*
> *I don't think she knew Dad was molesting me*
> *but I thought if I let him do it to me*
> *that my little sister would be ok." Margaret*

Margaret was the older of two sisters. She became somewhat of a substitute wife, preparing meals, watching after her sister and cleaning house. Mom left Margaret for long periods of time with dad, not knowing he was molesting her.

When Margaret learned her younger sister had also been sexually abused by dad, Margaret was crushed.

Margaret believed she had sacrificed herself to save her sister from the abuse as well as rescue her mom from more anger and stress. Margaret said she never told her mom because her mom wouldn't have been able to handle it.

It is precisely mom's focus on filling her own emptiness that blinds her to her daughter's pain, even to the point she is unable to see when her daughter is being abused by others.

While writing this book, I met Tiffany and Sarah, two friends who are trying to help each other through hard times.

Tiffany had her first child at age 16 and now, at age 21, has 4 kids. Her kids are in foster care, spread across the states living with different family members. She is staying in a one-bedroom apartment with her dad, who has cancer and is raising 3 sons.

"Tiffany, where's your mom?" She died when Tiffany was 2 years old. Dad remarried the wicked step-mom and then step-mom walked out when Dad was diagnosed with cancer, leaving Dad and their three sons.

Sarah's story was a little different. She made the mistake of storming out of the house after an argument with an abusive husband. Husband locked her out of the house and called his father, an attorney, and started divorce proceedings. Ex-husband now has the house and full custody of the kids. Sarah has no money, no family, no job, no car, and no place to live.

"Sarah, where's your mom?" Mom's a crackhead addict; dad is in prison; end of story.

Barely holding back my own tears, I prayed for them, hugging and whispering words of hope. I made sure they had dinner and gave them gas money to get back to Tiffany's house because Sarah was now staying with Tiffany, her sick dad and three brothers in the one-bedroom apartment.

And then there's Raelynn, a teen girl we have known for some time. She now wants to be called "Ray." She has bound her breasts tight to her chest with gauze, wearing sagging jeans and a long-sleeve plaid shirt. She's taking "T" (short for testosterone) and contemplating having her breasts removed, "it just hurts too much to be a girl."

All three girls were molested sometime in their youth and all three had unavailable fathers and physically or emotionally absent moms. None of them could ever imagine wearing a superwoman cape and conquering the world. They can barely conquer the day.

These stories are not unusual of today's young girls. They represent a generation of motherless daughters growing up as absent, dysfunctional women and mothers.

Many years ago I heard a variation of the following story on a popular radio broadcast...

A little girl, Angie, ran outside to help mom plant the newly purchased garden flowers. Angie grabbed the hand shovel and started digging, slinging dirt in the air, some landing in mom's hair!

Mom grabbed Angie's arm, pulling the gardening

tool from her and yelling, "Angie, go inside until I finish."

Mom turned her attention back to her plants. Angie stood and watched through the porch screen. Mom gently removed each delicate plant from it's container, rearranging the soil and tucking the tiny flowers in their new fresh beds.

"Mom, can I help?"

"Angie, NO! Not now," mom spouted, never looking Angie's direction.

"Mom..."

"What now, Angie?"

"Mom, do you love me as much as you do your flowers?"

Abuse is the exploitation or neglect of basic human needs. It can be defined as wrongful, unreasonable, or harmful treatment by word or deed. A child who is trapped in an abusive situation is like a prisoner of war with no power, no leverage, and no voice.

*Abuse deprives us of basic human needs ~*

❖ Survival (food, shelter, clothing)
❖ Safety (physical, emotional)
❖ Touching, skin contact
❖ Attention
❖ Mirroring and echoing

- ❖ Guidance
- ❖ Listening
- ❖ Participating
- ❖ Acceptance
- ❖ Opportunity to grieve losses and to grow
- ❖ Support
- ❖ Loyalty and trust
- ❖ Accomplishment
- ❖ Sexuality
- ❖ Enjoyment or fun
- ❖ Freedom
- ❖ Nurturing
- ❖ Unconditional love, including connection with God

Words are powerful. The writer of Proverbs 15:4 says, *"The tongue that brings healing is a tree of life, but a deceitful tongue crushes the spirit."*

Emotional abuse demeans a person's character and dignity and assaults self-esteem. *"Sticks and stones may break my bones, but names will never hurt me"* just isn't true. A child's world can be built by words of encouragement and acceptance or destroyed by cruel, demeaning words. Neglect—the absence of words, time, or touch—leaves a child emotionally hungry, literally starved for attention.

Types of emotional abuse include name calling, criticism, unrealistic expectations, absence of affection, not seeing the person's heart, not listening or affirming, belittling, blaming, and embarrassment.

Physical abuse results in bruises, black eyes, and broken bones; sometimes even death. Every blow causes damage to a person's dignity.

Punishing (inflicting harm through anger), rather than disciplining (training to bring about correction), is abusive treatment. The child is left confused, unable to understand the parent's action.

Physical abuse can range from withholding meals or other necessities of life to violent and unpredictable outbursts. Often moms slap their children in the face as a method of humiliation, which can wound deeper than the physical pain. Children raised in physically abusive homes often learn to inflict harm to control people and situations.

Mother-daughter abuse wounds daughter's hearts and souls. Their mothers were often their only caregivers and the only source of much-needed care.

Once a woman becomes aware of her own daughter's abuse, her fear, guilt and shame are reinforced through her failure to protect her own children.

> *"I'm yelling at my daughter just like*
> *my mom yelled at me.*
> *I'll tell her awful things and be so angry, then storm*
> *off and feel horrible for what I said or did." Andrea*

Andrea's mom was verbally and physically abusive to her, withholding affection or attention if Andrea didn't meet mom's expectations. Andrea promised herself she'd never be like her mom. Then, there she was, screaming one minute and looking at her kids with frowned brows of disapproval, withdrawing all attention and affection.

> *"I told my mom about the abuse and she never said any-*
> *thing. She kept looking at the dishes and cried.*
> *I realized then it was all still about her." Leslie*

Leslie's mom said she was sorry for being a bad mom but continued doing the dishes and never looked at her.

> **"I thought that part of my life was over,**
> **then my daughter gets abused.**
> **I don't get it...how did this happen?" Marie**

Marie is Leslie's mom. They wanted to reconcile their relationship but Marie admitted she never dealt with her own abusive past. She felt she could move on and just forget about it but her life was in constant chaos.

Marie frequently left her daughter, Leslie, with babysitters, not returning home until morning. Marie first learned of her daughter's sexual abuse when a teacher reported her concerns but never followed up on helping her daughter.

We may worry about replicating the dysfunction from our past but a grown daughter's unfulfilled emptiness is a set-up to continue a destructive cycle. We must proactively choose to learn differently so new patterns can develop.

Acknowledging and surrendering our mistakes and wrong choices to the Lord is the first step in healing. Surrender is a fruit of forgiveness and the heart that surrenders easily forgives.

Forgiveness is no longer hanging onto the circumstance or person(s) who hurt you. Forgiveness releases you from unforgiveness, a death grip on emotional pain. If you need more help understanding about surrender or forgiveness, refer to the two corresponding chapters in my book, *Dancing on the Graves of Your Past*. These are excellent resources to help with this important step in letting go of painful experiences.

To better understand mother-daughter patterns and the dysfunctional roots of a family cycle, construct a family tree outlining generational patterns and identifying the psychological, social, physical and spiritual profiles of your mom, grandma, and great-grandma. Also note any diseases or illness. If no longer alive, note the cause of death. Some answers can be found by looking at the beliefs and attitudes of the primary men in their lives. Then connect the dots to see her responses, reactions and behavior.

Dysfunctional cycles pass down from generation to generation. Look up and read Exodus 34:7 and Numbers 14:18. Ask God to show you what you may be inheriting through generational and "learned" beliefs and behaviors from your family.

When you repent on behalf of past generation's behavior and actions and break the generational patterns, you are cutting off, in the spirit, an ungodly and unholy alliance to a person or situation. Whether you were aware of this or not, these connections can take precedence and establish strongholds against freedom. Harmful generational patterns predispose you to these same strongholds.

When you surrender, forgive, and break negative generational patterns by receiving Jesus' atonement and redemption, you align yourself for blessing and prosperity as in Psalm 112:2, "His children will be mighty in the land; the generation of the upright will be blessed."

When we become part of God's family through Jesus, we receive our true spiritual inheritance and begin establishing Godly boundaries and new patterns of managing our freedom.

*"I pray also that the eyes of your heart may be enlightened in order that you may know the hope to which he has called you, the riches of his glorious inheritance in the saints, and his incomparably great power for us who believe. That power is like the working of his mighty strength, which he exerted in Christ when he raised him from the dead and seated him at his right hand in the heavenly realms, far above all rule and authority, power and dominion, and every title that can be given, not only in the present age but also in the one to come." Ephesians 1:18-21*

# 4

## Beyond Words

*"... Jesus said, "She is not dead but asleep."*
—*Luke 8:52*

Sexual abuse hurts a child no matter who the perpetrator is or how long it continued. Sexual abuse perpetrators are typically thought to be male, but not always. I consistently hear reports of sexual abuse by sisters, female babysitters, aunts, female neighbors and mothers.

Healing from any type of sexual abuse has its own set of hurdles to overcome, but sexual abuse perpetrated by females defies everything we believe, or want to believe, about women and especially mothers.

Most people don't want to believe that female perpetrators of sexual abuse exist and certainly don't want to believe that a mother could sexually abuse her own children. Mother-daughter sexual abuse is an uncomfortable subject and still a very taboo topic to discuss.

In general, people are far more outraged when they hear about mother-daughter sexual abuse than with father-daughter sexual abuse because a female sexual perpetrator violates the social expectations of women and mothers. Sadly, this reaction also points to how little we expect of men and fathers and establishes an unspoken standard that keeps women abusers ashamed and fearful from seeking help.

> *"I had a few flashbacks but kept ignoring what I remembered. I never knew anyone else who had been sexually abused by their mom. I mean, how do you tell someone your mom had sex with you?" Emily*

Emily's concerns and feelings about what happened to her made it difficult for her to even admit what her mom did. As she recounted the story of her abuse, she couldn't look up at me, wiping her eyes with the cuff of her sweater. Emily's pain was buried in feelings of shame and guilt, anger and sadness.

In a summary entitled *Mother Daughter Sexual Abuse* (Kali Munro, M.Ed., Psychotherapist, 2000), Kali tells us that daughters tend to be very confused and conflicted about abuse and more so when sexually abused by their mothers, especially when their mothers were their primary caregivers.

Daughters have a lot invested in *not* acknowledging that the abuse happened because daughters hold the same basic beliefs that society and the church holds about mothers. That is, mothers are all kind, loving and nurturing. It is very hard to accept that the very person who carried you through pregnancy and gave birth to you has sexually abused you.

When survivors of mother-daughter incest are able to acknowledge the abuse they experienced, they often believe that there must be something terribly wrong or bad about them. "How could my own mother sexually abuse me?"

Believing that all moms are caring and nurturing, a daughter feels that there is something really bad about the child whose mother would sexually abuse her.

> *"The first time it happened I was confused*
> *but after that I thought it must be my fault because*
> *it kept happening." Sue*

As with most sexual abuse, it was easier for Sue to believe that the abuse was her fault than to admit that a person who was supposed to love and protect her actually harmed her.

For both sexually abusive mothers and sexually abused daughters, it is extremely difficult to acknowledge the abuse because there are very few places that survivors can hear or read about mother-daughter incest, or even about female perpetrators.

> *"I can't believe she'd do something so disgusting.*
> *Didn't she know I'd remember and hate her for it?*
> *Do you think that makes me a lesbian?" Sarah*

Sarah told me she was sick to her stomach every time she thought what her mom had done to her, keeping the dark secret hidden for years. Prior to our meeting she has never talked about what happened between her and her mother.

Sarah hardly had words to describe what happened. It was a great struggle for her to label her experience as abuse. She feared that the incest was lesbian sex; something "dirty," not to be talked about or admitted.

"Do you think this makes me a lesbian?" Sarah asked. Sarah was afraid, if she told, she may be perceived as lesbian, or afraid that the abuse made her a lesbian.

Being abused by her mother does not make a survivor a lesbian even if the survivor's body physiologically responded to sensual or sexual stimulation. This is true with any sexual abuse.

The body's response to stimulation has nothing to do with sexuality. It is the body's natural physiological response and has nothing to do with the survivor's own sexual desires, or even consent. Sexual abuse may affect a survivor's comfort level with, and responses to, being a sexual person, but it does not cause her sexuality.

When sexual abuse triggers sensuality or pleasurable body responses, a feeling of pleasure and disgust can co-mingle. Deep feelings of self-hate often develop, believing their body's pleasurable response was a betrayal, "How can something so horrible not feel bad?"

Survivors of mother-daughter incest struggle to make sense of and understand their experience. Even when survivors acknowledge sexual abuse by their mothers, they often strongly identify with, and protect, their mothers. This identification with the perpetrator can make it more difficult for survivors to separate themselves, emotionally and otherwise, from their mothers.

Survivors of mother-daughter sexual abuse often see their future as a woman and mother as dismal. They can feel that they are untrustworthy, even reluctant to have children of their own.

> *"When I became pregnant I begged God to please NOT let me have a girl.*
> *I didn't feel safe with little girls.*
> *I was afraid they wouldn't be safe with me.*
> *I'd never want any little girl to experience the pain and hurt I had gone through." Natalie*

When Natalie found out she was pregnant, she prayed over and over asking God to please let her have a son. She was terrified of her ability to parent a daughter, worried her daughter would be victimized like she had been.

Daughters often look to their mother's experiences as a parallel for their future and may identify with their mother as a victim. If their mother is in an upsetting situation, daughters will often feel empathy for their mothers, and want to help them. This is heightened for a daughter whose mother sexually abused her, then turned to her for support.

The mixture of maternal care and sexual abuse leaves a daughter confused. Some survivors respond to these feelings by not wanting to be women or anything associated with mothering. On the one hand, she desperately needed to be loved, held, kissed, and nurtured, but that nurturance came with such a high price.

*Victims of mother-daughter sexual abuse tend to have heightened difficulties with ~*

* ❖ Naming their experience as abuse. This is particularly true in light of the myth that women do not sexually abuse children.

* ❖ Identity. Many survivors have difficulty knowing that they are separate and different than their mothers.

* ❖ Boundaries. Many survivors have difficulty maintaining their boundaries, especially with other

women. They may be overly flexible or overly rigid.

❖ Self-blame. Many survivors blame themselves. This self-blame is heightened in a cultural context where mothers are believed to be all loving and caring. It can't be the mother's fault, the thinking goes, so it must be theirs. They must be really bad if their own mother abused them.

❖ Gender identity. Many survivors have trouble identifying as women, or do not like what they perceive women to be, because the abuser was a woman and because the abuse focused on their female body. They know they are women, but in their minds being a woman is associated with being a victim, and/or being sexualized, "less than", or weak, etc.

❖ Gender shame. Many survivors feel great shame about being a woman because of their identification with their mothers as a perpetrator of the abuse. They feel that they are guilty of something and that it has to do with being female.

❖ Body shame. Survivors often feel great shame about their bodies, particularly their bodies' womanliness, both because their abuser had a woman's body and the abuse focused on their female body.

❖ <u>Fears about one's actual or perceived sexuality.</u> Survivors are often very confused about the differences between sexual abuse and sexuality, and may believe the myth that abuse causes a survivor's sexuality. This can lead to confusion about their sexuality and how others perceive their sexuality.

❖ <u>Longing to be loved.</u> Survivors frequently have a profound need to be loved in the way that they were not as a child, and they may fear or be unable to accept it, particularly from other women.

When you read this information about female sexual abuse, there may be a tendency to relate any other type of abuse, in contrast, as minor or less damaging. In reality, any type of sexual abuse may damage a person irrespective of duration, who the offender was, or the level of interaction.

> *"I guess I should be grateful it wasn't worse.*
> *This has happened to lots of people, right?" MaryAnn*

I like what Larry Crabb, professional counselor and author, said during one of his seminars…*"The size of the gun doesn't determine if you have been shot."* It is unfair to require a label be given to an event before feelings can be validated.

The lack of validation or concern from others perpetuates the need to hang on to the memory in an effort to be believed. In contrast, if a painful experience is denied, a type of emotional anorexia can develop protecting the person from any feelings at all.

In the aftermath of sexual abuse many women report feeling disconnected and emotionally dead. Words of sorrow or empathy do not heal sexual brokenness. Only the power of God's love can mend the emptiness and built a bridge to our future.

I love the story of Jairus' daughter in the Gospel of Luke 8:41-54. Jairus' requested Jesus come and heal his daughter who was ill. By the time Jesus arrived at Jairus' home, everyone was crying because, from all outward appearances, the daughter had died.

Jesus led the faithful past the faithless and went into the room where the daughter lay. He made a declaration..."*she is not dead, but asleep!*" Jesus followed up the declaration with a prophetic act, grasping her hand and telling her to get up!

God pushes past the unbelievers, those who hurt us and those who gave up on us. He pushes beyond our past and pain, and, as His daughters, declares we are not dead, just asleep.

Is there a part of you needs to be awakened to life?
Reach out and take Him by the hand and get up from a
place of slumber and sadness.

**Arise!**

**Believe in Him.**
**Believe in yourself.**

# 5

## Uncovered

*"Those who look to him are radiant;*
*their faces are never covered with shame."*
**—Psalm 34:5**

Wounded daughters feel betrayed, rejected, and abandoned by the parent(s) they loved and trusted. While some daughters were told outright that they were not okay – that they were stupid, bad, or undeserving – other daughters concluded that there was something wrong with them by the way they were being treated.

Not feeling seen, loved, valued, or understood can develop the belief there was something wrong with us.

This is the essence of shame; the belief there is something intrinsically wrong with **you**. Whereas guilt is about *doing* something wrong, shame is about *being* wrong at the core of who you are; flawed, inadequate, wrong, bad, unimportant, undeserving, or not good enough, often with no hope of it ever changing.

> *"I carried shame everywhere I went. It was like I had a huge X-type mark on me and everyone could see it and judged me." Susan*

Shame attached with abuse and trauma, like in Susan's case, is a profound sense of unworthiness, feeling defective or flawed. Shame exposes the fear of being uncovered or unprotected and feelings of "less than."

Hope-less

Power-less

Help-less

Use-less

Worth-less

Feeling-less

## Feelings of shame can lead to ~

- ❖ Feeling ashamed believing abuse or trauma experience was your fault and unable to forgive yourself.

- ❖ Enduring physical or emotional pain most people would not accept.

- ❖ Avoiding mistakes "at any cost."

- ❖ Feeling that you should be punished for the trauma event.

- ❖ Feeling bad when something good happens.

- ❖ Having suicidal thoughts, threats and attempts.

- ❖ Avoiding safe relationships that are self-nurturing and feel good.

- ❖ Perceiving others always as better, happier and more competent.

- ❖ Feeling unworthy, unlovable, immoral or sinful because of experiences.

- ❖ Inadequate and negative self images.

- ❖ Confusion and shame about being a woman.

- ❖ Uncomfortable with your sexuality.

- ❖ Engaging in self-injurious behavior (particularly in the genital and breast area), cutting and self-mutilation.

- ❖ Developing addictive patterns.

- ❖ Developing disordered eating.

❖ Experiencing body shame.

❖ Difficulties in relationships.

> *"I have always been ashamed of being overweight,*
> *but honestly, eating was the only way*
> *I could deal with all the anger."* **Morgan**

## *Shame has a purpose and serves us in several ways ~*

❖ Shame gives us a feeling of control over other people's feelings and behavior.

❖ Shame protects us from other feelings that we are afraid to acknowledge or feel, and gives us a sense of control over our own feelings.

❖ Shame will postpone the natural grief process which is important in good emotional health.

As long as we believe that we are the cause of other's rejecting behavior, then we can believe that there is something we can do about it. It gives us a sense of power to believe that others are rejecting us or behaving in unloving ways because of our inadequacy.

If what happened is our fault, then maybe we can do something about it by changing ourselves or by doing things "right." We hang on to the belief that our inadequacy is causing others' behavior because we don't want to accept other's free will to feel and behave however they want. We don't want to accept our helplessness over another's feelings and behavior.

When we can admit our responsibility for a situation, we can seek forgiveness and change our heart. When we believe something is our fault and we were *not responsible*, we take ownership of other people's behavior and actions.

Feeling something was your fault when it isn't, promotes the underlying belief that you are powerful enough to control others. After all, if you are at fault, you must be in charge and therefore have the power to make others behave in certain ways. This false belief is not only harmful to us, but it also relieves others from taking responsibility for their own actions.

It is important for you to ask the Lord, "Who is responsible or who is at fault?"

- ❖ Take responsibility if it is your fault, repent and ask forgiveness, forgiving yourself when needed.
- ❖ Refuse responsibility if it is not your fault, handing back the responsibility for the actions of others and forgive.

* Break agreement with any ungodly or unholy bonding, including agreement with shame, fear, or control.

* Come out of partnership with "it's my fault."

As bad as shame feels, many people prefer it to the feelings that shame may be covering up – loneliness, sadness, sorrow, rejection, abandonment, or betrayal. Just as anger may be a cover-up for these difficult feelings, so is shame.

---

*"When my dad died, I just couldn't process the loss. Most of my day was consumed with feelings of shame because I didn't have a dad." Natalie*

---

Many people would rather feel the awful feeling of shame than the authentic painful feelings resulting from a traumatic or abusive experience.

Loneliness, sadness, and sorrow are natural responses to circumstances. Grief is the emotional processing of loss, particularly loss of someone or something to which a bond was formed. The term "bereavement" often refers to the state of loss, and grief to the reaction of loss.

Although focused on the emotional response to loss, grief also has physical, cognitive, behavioral, social, and philosophical dimensions. Losses can range from loss of one's home, employment, financial status, a sense of safety, order, or possessions, the loss of family, friends and even pets.

I also recognized personally the need to grieve the loss of innocent childhood, creativity and dreams.

## You will heal from shame when you ~

❖ Are willing to accept that you are not responsible for another's feelings and behavior.

❖ Accept that others have free will to be open or closed, loving or unloving - that you are not the cause of their feelings and behavior and you no longer take responsibility for others' behavior.

❖ Let go of your need to control others and instead move into forgiveness and compassion for others.

❖ Are willing to be present with your authentic feelings and embrace the process of grief.

❖ Come out of agreement with needing shame as a covering and control mechanism.

When you let go of false beliefs about yourself, the roots to feeling of shame, you will no longer have a need to protect against these feelings with blame or shame.

If you are finding it difficult to move beyond shame, it is because you may be committed to the feeling of control that shame-based beliefs offer – control over others' feelings and behavior and control over your own authentic suppressed feelings.

> *"Feeling ashamed held me back from engaging in social activities. If I didn't reach out and meet people, no one could reject me." Cynthia*

Cynthia's shame was a type of control. As long as she was ashamed she could control her fear of being rejected in relationships. Shame and control are intricately tied together. As long as having the control is most important to you, you will not let go of shame. When you give up your attachment to control and instead choose forgiveness and compassion toward yourself and others, you will find shame disappearing.

Allies that hold shame in place are the "anti-self" beliefs such as self-rejection, self-pity and self-judgment, frequently leading to self-hate.

Compulsive "anti-self" feelings are merciless and destructive and can lead to self damage like mutilation, cutting or placing yourself in exploitive, dangerous or high-risk situations.

> *"When I began to heal I realized all the years I hated my dad, I was actually hating myself."*
> **Maggie**

Praying with Maggie to separate herself from dad's abuse was a huge step in Maggie accepting herself.

We have attributes, good and bad, direct and inherited, from both mother and father. Being angry, disappointed or hating either one of them will spill over into your own self-image.

I had the wonderful opportunity to sit under the ministry of Henry Wright, well-respected minister and author of *A More Excellent Way.* Henry Wright is considered highly knowledgeable and gifted in the area of physical and emotional healing and his material is used as a primary reference for most healing room ministries.

Henry teaches that self-hate, self-rejection, self-resentment, self-unforgiveness, and other "anti-self" issues are one of the major sources of many physical and mental health problems.

In *A More Excellent Way*, Henry writes the following concerning diseases such as Lupus, Crohn's, diabetes, rheumatoid arthritis, and MS:

> *"The body attacks the body because the person is attacking themselves spiritually in self-rejection, self-hatred, and self-bitterness. There is a spiritual dynamic that comes in which the white corpuscles are invisibly redirected to attack living tissue while ignoring the true enemy which is bacteria and viruses."*

In other words, auto-immune diseases are responses where the body attacks its living tissues as a result of the person attacking themselves through extreme self-hated, self-bitterness, and self-rejection.

I had opportunity to ask Henry about sugar addiction. I was curious because both my mother and my uncle, as recovering alcoholics, ate an enormous amount of candy. Henry explained that alcohol turns to sugar in the body so consuming both sugar and alcohol has the self-soothing purpose and both addictions are rooted in abandonment.

Consider the following speech attributed to Nelson Mandela after being released as a prisoner of war.

*"Our deepest fear is not that we are inadequate.*
*Our deepest fear is that we are powerful beyond measure.*
*It is our light, not our darkness, that most frightens us.*
*We ask ourselves, who am I to be brilliant, gorgeous, talented,*
*and fabulous? Actually, who are you not to be? You are a child*
*of God. Your playing small doesn't serve the world.*
*There's nothing enlightened about shrinking so that other*
*people won't feel insecure around you. We are all meant to*
*shine, as children do. We are born to make manifest the glory*
*of God that is within us. It's not just in some of us, it's in*
*everyone. And as we let our own light shine, we unconsciously*
*give other people permission to do the same.*
*As we are liberated from our own fear, our presence*
*automatically liberates others."*

For many of us that speech content feels like a contradiction, simply because for most of us our greatest fear is that we are inadequate, helpless and of no consequence in the grand scheme of life. Our negativity is self-destructive. Love and hope lead us forward towards continuing growth and understanding of ourselves and accordingly, others around us.

Without hope, life is darkness. Darkness is fear and bigotry, the road to self-destruction and denial of all our human virtues. If severe enough, it leads to our soul going to sleep for self-protection.

"Surely the darkness will hide me and the light become night around me, even the darkness will not be dark to you; the night will shine like the day, for darkness is as light to you. For you created my inmost being; you knit me together in my mother's womb. I praise you because I am fearfully and wonderfully made; your works are wonderful, I know that full well. My frame was not hidden from you when I was made in the secret place. When I was woven together in the depths of the earth, your eyes saw my unformed body.

All the days ordained for me were written in your book before one of them came to be. How precious to me are your thoughts, O God! How vast is the sum of them! Were I to count them, they would outnumber the grains of sand. When I awake, I am still with you." Psalm 139: 11-18

6

## Confused Love

*"Such love has no fear because perfect love expels all fear. If we are afraid, it is for fear of judgment, and this shows that his love has not been perfected in us. "*
—*1 John 4:18*

Shame convicts us of judgment and breeds confusion where love is concerned. When shame is present, it is an indication there may be an "orphan heart" as Jesus addressed in John, chapter 14. The orphaned heart feels alone, unprotected and unable to depend on others and shame is the result of believing we are inadequate.

In this chapter of John, Thomas questioned Jesus and His promise He would not leave them, but would return to them. Jesus tells Thomas and the disciples *"I will not leave you as orphans...."*

In recognition of Thomas response, Jesus discerns an "orphan" spirit manifested in Thomas' *fear* of being left alone, unprotected, uncovered, rejected and abandoned. Fear is at the root of the orphan heart.

> *"As soon as I heard Dad's car come into the driveway, panic filled my heart. I would wait by the window to see if he was angry or drunk. Either way it was the beginning of another long night." Norma*

The fear Norma experienced was traumatic. Fear can be described as an unpleasant, strong emotion caused by anticipation or awareness of danger. For Norma, the fear began as soon as she heard her dad arrive home. Her adrenaline would peak causing what we would call a panic attack, a response to the experience of trauma.

Fear acts like an alarm in recognition and response to dangerous situations and pending threats, the worsening of a situation, or continuation of a situation that is unacceptable.

Remember the days when we would keep new-born babies wrapped up tightly in receiving blankets? The point was to keep baby feeling safe as they adjusted to freedom outside the close-knit proximity of the womb. When baby cried, arms and legs wildly flailing in the air, we'd wrap up (swaddle) our baby and hold them close to our chest to console and comfort.

Captured by fear, we desperately strive, searching for someone to wrap up and hold us close, safe and warm.

Think about this in context of the following poem from John and Paula Sanford's book, 1982, *The Transformation of the Inner Man.*

*I'm not the same on the outside*
*as I am on the inside.*
*I smile, I laugh*
*but I don't know joy.*
*Where is my joy, O my God?*
*Why have you forsaken me?*
*Everything was once so free...*
*Once grass was green,*
*and hills were pretty.*
*Now I seem to see them through*
*a veil of grey.*
*Inside is cold and tight and sad.*
*I cry and ache.*

Most days I long for eyes to see me.

But I hide so well, none can see.

I know it's me but then I think,

They don't care – He must not care.

But too long I have known His love,

And I know this is not true.

I am unable to get above

and I am sinking slowly in the sands.

"Help," I say – inside I scream –

but on my face, I smile.

Only my eyes express – the well

of pain in me.

I'm careful not to look at those

who might strip away my mask.

But I want it to come down, at last

reality to grasp.

I cannot do this for myself.

Am I ready for You at last?

"Honesty," we cry,

"transparency," and the like.

But who will brave this scary turf?

I've been there, I've tried.

But from openness came pain, from

those who want to close my door,

who trample my little girl.

*So light and gay is she, but oh, so sensitive,*

*too many times others have driven her in.*

*"Come out, little girl," I coax,*

*But she just sits and mopes.*

*No longer can I coax her out.*

*Are you sleeping, little girl?*

*Lord, send someone to love her to*

*life, once more.*

Paul, in Romans 8:38-39, writes, *"For I am convinced that neither death nor life, neither angels nor demons, neither the present nor the future, nor any powers, neither height nor depth, nor anything else in all creation, will be able to separate us from the love of God that is in Christ Jesus our Lord."*

Paul mentions the present and the future, but he doesn't mention the past. The past can't separate you from God's love because He sent Jesus, His love incarnate, to redeem the past. But the past *can* separate you from the awareness of God's love.

> *"After the sexual assault, I felt damaged,*
> *alone and afraid.*
> *I thought God must love everyone but me." Carrie*

After Carrie was date-raped, she reported it to the police but had no one to help her cope in the months following the assault. She turned to her church family but they were judgmental and told her she needed to forgive and put it all behind her. Carrie said she tried to pray but felt isolated and alone believing God was uncaring and unavailable.

Jesus promised He wouldn't leave the disciples as orphans, alone and fearful, but would send them the Holy Spirit called the Spirit of Truth (John 14:17.) The Holy Spirit is also referred to as the comforter and counselor.

Jesus sent us truth, comfort, and counsel in the form of the Holy Spirit, who would be both *with* and *inside* us, to wrap us up and keep us safe and warm.

He reminds us of the Holy Spirit's presence when He tells us in *Matthew 28:20* "...*surely I am with you always, to the very end of the age.*"

Isaiah 41:13 *"For I am the Lord, your God, who takes hold of your right hand and says to you, Do not fear; I will help you."*

Romans 8:15 *"For you did not receive a spirit that makes you a slave again to fear, but you received the Spirit of son-ship. And by him we cry, "Abba, Father."*

Proverbs 10:12 *"... but love covers over all wrongs."*

God not only gives love but IS love and we are made in His image. Within us, created in our DNA is the capacity to give and receive love.

> *"When I said 'I love you', it was really an invitation for them to say they loved me, too. I'd say I loved them just to hear them say they still loved me but even if they said it, I wouldn't believe it." Alice*

Relationships were always one-sided for Alice. She loved too much, too fast, choosing men who ended up emotionally or physically hurting her.

Alice grew up deprived of unconditional love. Children deprived of love may seek it throughout their adult lives – in ways very dangerous to themselves and to others. Love between adults requires earned or maintained behavior, that is, love is usually conditional.

When our desperate need to be loved isn't filled, less worthy things can attempt to replace authentic love.

Intensity keeps adrenaline at peak performance. Like a car's gas pedal at full throttle increasing the RPM of an engine, fear releases a "fight or flight" fuel into the brain keeping adrenaline at full throttle and in control.

Fear will consistently and persistently press you into a state of tension and stress. Like shame, fear can become protective and controlling.

Using drugs, alcohol or even sex as an attempt to de-escalate from intensity is the set up for addiction; the satiation of a self-medicated state that temporarily brings a sense of relief.

---

*"When he hit me, he'd say it was my fault.*
*Later he would say he was sorry and hold me.*
*I wanted him to hold me without hitting me first but it*
*never worked out that way." Sarah*

---

Sarah was involved in a violent marriage. The cycle of abuse always ended with her husband crying, saying he was sorry and holding her in ways she always wanted. She endured long seasons of abuse to get to those few moments. However, as the years went by, the severity of abuse escalated until one night he hit her so hard she passed out.

Relationships that are about insane loyalty or attachment share aspects of exploitation, risk, fear and danger. They may also have elements of kindness or nobility. Often there is seduction, deception or betrayal.

Women involved in relationships that include elements of trauma such as fear, betrayal, deception, exploitation, danger, risk, and terror, often mistake intensity for intimacy.

Sometimes emotional pain, severe consequences and even the prospect of death does not stop commitment and caring within intensity-based relationships.

---

*"The house was always a mess and everyone was stressed and screaming at each other.*
*Mom drank and overdosed on pills and Dad yelled at her while the ambulance guy was trying to help her.*
*It was always crazy but that was normal for us."*
*Maggie*

---

Through our ministry time together, Maggie began to realize "crazy" was normal and that she continued to pursue relationships that were equally as intense.

Dysfunctional attachments occur in the presence of intensely-bonded relationships.

Ungodly and unholy bonds are created when intensity is substituted for intimacy. Ungodly or unholy bonding includes inability to detach and self-destructive denial. All ungodly and unholy bonding is idolatry and misplaced loyalty.

## Indicators of ungodly and unholy bonding ~

❖ When everyone around you has strong negative reactions, yet you continue covering up, defending, or explaining a relationship.

❖ When there is a constant pattern of nonperformance and yet you continue to believe false promises.

❖ When there are repetitive, destructive fights that nobody wins.

❖ When others are horrified by something that has happened to you and you are not.

❖ When you obsess over showing someone that he or she is wrong about you, your relationship, or the person's treatment of you.

❖ When you feel stuck because you know what the other person is doing is destructive to you, but believe you cannot do anything about it.

❖ When you feel loyal to someone even though you harbor secrets that are damaging to them.

- ❖ When you move closer to someone you know is destructive to you with the desire of converting them to a non-abuser.
- ❖ When someone's talents, charisma or contributions cause you to overlook destructive, exploitive or degrading acts.
- ❖ When you cannot detach from someone even though you do not trust, like, or care for the person.
- ❖ When you find yourself missing, *even to the point of nostalgia and longing,* a relationship so awful it almost destroyed you.
- ❖ When extraordinary demands are placed upon you to measure up as a way to cover up that you've been exploited.
- ❖ When you keep secret someone's destructive behavior toward you because of all the good they have done or the importance of their position or career.
- ❖ When the history of your relationship is about contracts or promises that have been broken and that you are asked to over- look.

*Situations where ungodly or unholy bonding is likely to occur ~*

- ❖ Incest and child abuse
- ❖ Consensual sex
- ❖ Non-consensual sex

- ❖ Dysfunctional marriages
- ❖ Domestic violence
- ❖ Co-dependency
- ❖ Addictions
- ❖ Exploitation in the workplace
- ❖ Agreements and partnerships
- ❖ Contracts
- ❖ Litigation
- ❖ Kidnapping
- ❖ Hostage situations
- ❖ Cults and occult
- ❖ Religious abuse

> *"Over and over my dad ignored me. It seemed the more he rejected me, the harder I tried to be pretty or smarter to win his approval. I was always manipulating to feel loved by him." Marsha*

Growing up with an absence of authentic love, Marsha, as an adult, bonded in loyalty to relationships that were essentially void of love. She repeatedly dated men who would exploit and manipulate her kindness.

Relationships void of authentic love cause us to feel rejected. Rejection partners with the belief we are not acceptable to another person. Rejection can lead us into performance as we try through behavior and works to gain approval of another person. Continuing down this path and holding onto rejection leads to idolatry where we focus more on other's opinions of us rather than God's opinion of us.

*Focusing on rejection leads to ~*

- ❖ Withdrawal or isolation
- ❖ Anger and hatred
- ❖ Jealousy and envy
- ❖ Perfectionism
- ❖ People pleasing
- ❖ Co-dependency
- ❖ Idolatry

Rejection leads to fear we are unlovable. Fear will cause us to self-protect and respond in unloving ways toward others, shielding our heart from the pain of others not loving us.

When we are unlovely towards our self and others, that is, behaving in unloving ways, we expose our deep need to be loved.

An unloving spirit exhibits the inability to give and receive authentic love. Its footprints are seen in family generations where there has been a history of rejection and abandonment, resulting in a problem with authentic intimacy and the absence of love demonstrated through time, attention or touch.

The unloving spirit promotes the anti-self feelings which (last chapter) are often the pre-cursers to auto-immune problems. Infirmity becomes a partner with the unloving spirit.

Andrew Vachss is a high-profile attorney who defends children who have been abused. Following is an excerpt from a Parade Magazine (March, 1996) article entitled *"Our Search for Love:"*

*"There is no such thing as a good baby or a bad baby
which is why love and protectiveness must
be unconditional for them all."*

*"I once represented a child who had been horribly tortured
by her mother. On the witness stand, the abuser (mom)
explained why she had burned the child by holding
her little hand against a hot stove grid;
'She wouldn't leave me alone.'*

*The child's crime was to follow her mother around the
house, attempting to wring from her the love she so desperately
needed. Slaps and kicks did not stop the child's search
for love, so mom decided more extreme measures
were needed to teach her a lesson.*

*Here is what I tell so many formerly abused children
who are now adults: Look how desperately you wanted to bond
with parents who would not love you. That is not a defect; indeed, it can be a strength. It proves that the ability to love
has not been eradicated in you…*

*When our biological families no longer function, the only*
*option is to create a family of choice – a family defined by*
*shared purpose and mutual respect, not ties of blood…*
*then you can have the family you need.*

*But that means to contribute not demand…*

*Yes, you were cheated and robbed of the unconditional*
*love you deserved as a child, but if you devote*
*your life to that theft,*
*you are doomed.*"

Any unlovely or unloving spirit may guard, deny, or reject love, but cannot remove the *capacity* for love created by God in us.

Clearly, it was the love of God through Jesus who set free the insane man filled with demons (Mark 5:15).

The demons may have violently manipulated and tortured the man but the legion of demons could not destroy the man's capacity for love. When Jesus set him free, love returned, conquered and filled him.

Interestingly, after the man was free, Jesus did not allow him to follow with Jesus and the disciples. For years the man had just been a prisoner of domination and control and Jesus refused to take the place of "legion." Instead, Jesus sent him back to his village to live with family and friends to learn how to steward his freedom through his own voice, choices and boundaries.

While we may reject God's love or deny Jesus' atonement for our shame, sickness, and sin, we cannot dismiss our need for love. No guard or barrier or demon can destroy love, which is the nature of God, created in us.

Love does not partner with shame, fear, rejection, abandonment or hate. It does not replicate the control of orphan-generated intensity in ungodly, unholy bonding and loyalty.

*"Love is patient, love is kind. It does not envy, it does not boast, it is not proud. It is not rude, it is not self-seeking, it is not easily angered, it keeps no record of wrongs.*
*Love does not delight in evil but rejoices with the truth.*
*It always protects, always trusts, always hopes,*
*always perseveres.*
*Love never fails."*
*1 Corinthians 13:4-8*

Love actually brings justice and demands (requires) protection. Those who are unable to give and receive love reject the work of the Cross and the Blood of Jesus and thereby reject the "love" God sent them.

Repentance and renouncing misplaced loyalty (ungodly and unholy allegiance) is no longer believing anything less than authentic love is worthy of our loyalty.

*The antidote for rejection, fear, and ultimately the unloving spirit is ~*

- ❖ Forgive those who were unable to give you what you needed.

- ❖ Ask God to forgive you for placing another's opinions of you in front of His.

- ❖ Renounce the lie that another person has the power to diminish you.

- ❖ Come out of agreement that others define who you are.

- ❖ Ask forgiveness if you rejected or hurt others.

- ❖ Re-establish your identity in the mirror of who God says you are, through His definition of you.

- ❖ Ask the Holy Spirit to fill you with His Presence, fullness and joy.

The best way to prevent child abuse is to be good to yourself...YOU are a child of the King!

Loving yourself is accepting yourself and believing you are worthy of good things from God.

# 7

## Spirituality & Sexuality

*"Flee from sexual immorality.*
*All other sins a man commits are outside his body,*
*but he who sins sexually sins against his own body."*
*—1Cor. 6:18*

Spirituality and sexuality may seem on opposite ends of the spectrum but God links the two together when he intertwines sexual and spiritual language with reference to our relationship to Him.

In Genesis, God shows us the correlation between our spirituality and sexuality. Ezekiel, Hosea and Song of

Songs are familiar books of the Bible where God uses sexual language to describe spiritual concepts.

Genesis 1:27,28 explains God created Adam both male and female. God gave the commission to Adam (actually God called Adam "them") to *be fruitful and increase in number, fill the earth and subdue it.*

God must have thought it would be boring for Adam to reproduce within himself so God removed Adam's rib and fashioned woman, a suitable helper, and now there were two persons. Pretty simple math!

Adam then prophesied in Genesis 2:23 *"This is now bone of my bones and flesh of my flesh; she shall be called 'woman,' for she was taken out of man."* Continuing in Genesis 2:24,25, *"For this reason a man will leave his father and mother and be united to his wife, and they will become one flesh. The man and his wife were both naked, and they felt no shame."*

In the paradise of Eden, before the fall, Adam and Eve were naked before God and were not ashamed. Perhaps Adam and Eve were unaware they were naked because they felt clothed in the reflection they saw of themselves through God's presence with them. It seems He covered them with the experience of His love and righteousness, producing innocence and holiness in their view and belief about themselves. They were created in His image and lived in the continual perfected image of God as they saw themselves through the mirror of His eyes.

When sin entered, Adam and Eve no longer saw their reflection in the image of God, rather they were awakened to their own image, form and body.

*"Then the eyes of both of them were opened, and they realized they were naked; so they sewed fig leaves together and made coverings for themselves.*

*Then the man and his wife heard the sound of the LORD God as he was walking in the garden in the cool of the day, and they hid from the LORD God among the trees of the garden.*

*But the LORD God called to the man, "Where are you?" He answered, "I heard you in the garden, and I was afraid because I was naked; so I hid."*

*And he said, "Who told you that you were naked?"* Gen 3:7-11

Adam and Eve, aware they were naked, no longer covered and clothed by God, became self-conscious. Self-consciousness produced fear of intimacy, and shame and perverted the innocence of our unclothed body.

Spirituality and sex were introduced before the serpent and sin. It doesn't take a rocket scientist to figure out that "two became one" is a picture of intimate spiritual union between Adam and Eve. Although sexual intercourse is not directly referred to in scripture prior to the entrance of sin, God proposed that a man and woman would come together in the pleasurable union of sexual intercourse to increase in number, producing children. Sexual relationship was part of God's paradise of blessing, fulfillment, reproduction and pleasure.

Spiritual oneness in sexual union represents the fullness and willingness for a man and woman to give all they are through their bodies to fulfill the other.

Marital sexual oneness is sanctioned and holy more than any other form of human experience. The body and soul response to sexual connection is basic physiology and psychology but the deeper connection is spiritual.

Eve, without hesitation or doubt, was to trust Adam to enter inside of her and unite with her. Although their bodies were naked, there was no shame because their union was to be covered and clothed by God. The union of Adam and Eve's bodies together as "one," fulfilled the spiritual completeness of Adam originally. While sexual union was the vehicle, it was not the goal. The goal was that Adam and Eve, together as one flesh, embody the fullness of God's image in mankind.

The marriage ceremony between man and woman is a prophetic act sanctioning their emotional, physical, and spiritual unity under God.

As a side note, the consummation of a marriage is fulfilled by an act of sexual intercourse between the spouses; the compliment (expression of esteem) and completion of their commitment to one another.

In today's terms, the absence of sexual union after marriage signifies the marriage was never consummated.

A Godly-instituted sexual union possesses the amazing power to bless, fulfill, and express love. To the contrary, when used destructively, it holds the power to harm, pervert and unleash devastation

Despite the decline of morality and increase in sexual promiscuity, most of society remains appalled and horrified by news and reports of rape, sex trafficking, sexual violence and exploitation. Inherent in our humanity is belief that violating the sexual integrity and dignity of another person is forbidden and prohibited.

The capacity to be sexual is initially formed in a girl as her spirit learns to find safety in the strength of her father's arms. As a child, she learns to rest, trust, and come alive in the healthy non-sexual embrace of the opposite gender. A daughter who is sexualized doesn't know what to do with that. Her body has not yet awakened to the season of unity in marriage.

A little girl will pretend to flirt, lure, cuddle up with, and practice innocent kisses and hugs with her dad. When Dad responds honorably with delight, he affirms and approves, nurturing her confidence and value. Through his responses to her, she learns how to trust a man.

If Dad dishonored her by ignoring, punishing, or misappropriating her innocent gestures of flirting, kissing, or cuddling, daughter may carry the blame and ultimate shame for Dad's disapproval of her.

> "*Dad bought me a blue dress and the first time*
> *I put it on, I twirled around to show it off.*
> *He pulled me on to his lap and molested me.*
> *Every time I wore the blue dress*
> *the same thing happened.*" *Jennifer*

Jennifer's father shattered the essence of what it means to be a father and ultimately for her to grow from daughter to wife. The hardest part of Jennifer's healing was forgiving herself for putting on the blue dress. "You don't understand," she told me, "sometimes I'd put on the dress just so he'd pay attention to me."

Dad carries the responsibility to nurture a daughter's femininity and sexuality as a physical representation of Father God's covering in holiness, cultivating her capacity to give herself in marriage. If Dad violates his responsibilities by sexualizing his daughter, he warps and perverts her delicate innocence and trust.

When I was little I loved to dance around and make my dad smile. At first, he'd smile and wink and I felt special but then he began making lewd gestures that made me uncomfortable. As an adult I realized he sexualized and exploited me. I was mostly angry with myself for all the times I danced in front of him. For many years I could never participate in worshipful dance at church until I forgave my dad and myself, letting go of carrying the responsibility of my dad's behavior.

Any form of sexual abuse is not only immoral, it is unloving and ungodly. Sexual exploitation or deviance including being disrespected, manipulated, sexualized, viewed, exposed to, lusted after, joked about, objectified, touched, pressured, assaulted, or violated disrupts a woman's trust, innocence and vulnerability.

> *"There were five of us sisters when my mom died.*
> *Each one of us took responsibility for the household chores.*
> *All of us took turns sleeping in Dad's bed.*
> *My sister still lives with him." Gina*

Sexual abuse started long before Gina's mom died but after mom's death, the daughters in Gina's family became surrogate wives and dad's sexual partners. One of Gina's sisters never married and still lives in the home taking care of her dad.

Gina was married with two young children and loved her husband very much but she froze and became non-responsive to his desire for sex. "It was like my heart loved him but my body closed up in protest."

When Gina complied and agreed to sex with her husband, the event would be flooded with recurring flashbacks of her dad and she would panic.

A daughter who is sexually abused can become confused with the union of her spirit to another as a mate. This ungodly and unholy union warps the intended trusted sanctity of a woman giving herself, through her body, to her husband.

Gina also disclosed that sometimes in the night she awoke feeling drawn, against her will, into a sexual encounter. She would feel this as a violation but also fought against feelings of being sexually attracted.

The enemy does not play fair and seeks every advantage to pervert Godly love and the holiness of sexual union. Like 220 volts of electricity into a 110 volt socket, sex is an experience a child has no capacity to negotiate or navigate.

Nighttime experiences surrounding sex are embarrassing to talk about perpetuating silence, confusion and shame. One symptom is waking in the night with heaviness on the chest and limited breathing, feeling held down. This can be a post-traumatic flashback from oral rape or a child being held down or laid upon during sexual abuse. Waking in the night with sexual thoughts or feelings of being sexually violated can be a post-traumatic flash where the past event floods into a present moment.

However, spiritual warfare is real and sometimes these symptoms are the result of what we would typically call a *nightmare*, a word derived from the demon *Mare*, who harasses during the night; a type of Nephilim as described in Genesis 6.

Spiritual night-visitor experiences that harm, seduce and violate are part of this category and usually result from witchcraft (personal or generational) combining spirits of darkness with sexual activity.

An experienced counselor can help you through to freedom. The following is not inclusive of all aspects associated with night visitors, rather is more of a directional overview for prayer.

*Steps to freedom may include renouncing, repenting and asking forgiveness for ~*

❖ Generational or personal experiences with occult activity.

❖ Generational or personal fornication, incest, homosexuality, sexual addiction, pornography, rape, masturbation, fantasy lust, bestiality, perversion or prostitution.

❖ Generational or personal soul bonding, misplaced loyalty, and idolatry; name, renounce, and break off each of the connections.

❖ All acts that included shedding of innocent blood, abortion, and murder.

❖ Ask Papa God to restore innocence.

If you feel you were the victim of SRA (satanic ritual abuse) there would be deeper prayer ministry needed.

When a husband and wife are sexually innocent and unite together as "one," there is no sexual history to disturb their unity. The cross-current of giving and taking is not compromised or distorted from prior sexual experiences. The inability to fully let go into sexual pleasure is often the result of prior sexual experiences that were damaging.

The casual use of sex with multiple partners institutes one flesh relationships whereby, after the relationship ends, our spirit searches over and over for the ones with whom we have united. The process of searching, but never finding, leaves an unfulfilled desire and longing, destroying trust in the spiritual foundation of true Godly union where the Glory of His image is reflected when two come together as one.

With each sexual partner, a woman opens herself to the generational spiritual history of that sexual partner. This is how generational behaviors, iniquity, and strongholds are passed down. I call them *spiritually transmitted diseases*. They are passed down to you from parents, grandparents, etc., and until broken, from you to your next generation.

*"You shall not bow down to them or worship them; for I, the LORD your God, am a jealous God, punishing the children for the sin of the fathers to the third and fourth generation of those who hate me," Exodus 20:5*

*"...maintaining love to thousands, and forgiving wickedness, rebellion and sin. Yet he does not leave the guilty unpunished; he punishes the children and their children for the sin of the fathers to the third and fourth generation." Exodus 34:7*

Prophetically speaking, what we see manifest in the physical realm is insight and revelation of what is happening in the spiritual realm. The world's current highlight on sex, sexuality, and sexual behavior screams to us about the consequences, specifically, the perversion of spirituality.

For females, there are only two ways she invites and allows anything to enter inside of her.

The first would be giving permission for the Holy Spirit to enter her through spiritual union and the second would be when she gives permission for a man to enter inside her through sexual union.

Trauma and betrayal pervert trust and fortify self-protective walls which surface even when intimate relationships are available. Sexual abuse and trauma bring increased shame and self-consciousness and cause a woman to have extreme difficulty trusting in deep spiritual relationships. This destructive cycle will contribute to NOT fully trusting God, Jesus, or the Holy Spirit.

As long as she is committed to protect herself and makes decisions that reinforce those beliefs, she will not rise up to the greater image of God which she was originally destined to carry.

Until she is healed and set free, the enemy will pull on fear and shame, lie and manipulate to keep her from wearing and carrying the holy image of God.

He, the enemy, will poke and pick at her nakedness (self-consciousness) and she will seek ways to cover her self; her body.

# 8

## What's A Girl To Do?

*"...you were bought at a price.*
*Therefore honor God with your body."*
*—1Cor 6:20*

Young Jenny's father is chasing her through the fields to beat her when she stops and hides, praying...

*"Dear God, make me a bird*
*so I could fly far....far, far away from here."*

As an adult, Jenny returns to the old house where she lived as a child with her abusive father.

Jenny, revisited by the trauma and abuse, picks up rocks throwing them with all her physical strength at the old house.

Forrest watches and remarks...

*"I guess sometimes there just aren't enough rocks."*

(Excerpt from the popular 1994 movie, Forrest Gump)

Jenny's life was surrounded by people of a questionable nature: a sexually-abusive father, an audience more interested in her naked body than her folk guitar solo, and an abusive hippie-boyfriend.

She wants to be famous and rich, but ends up with dead beat jobs and emotionally unavailable men, using drugs and talking about suicide. She wants love, but can't receive love from the one (Forrest) who is close by and truly cares for her.

Jenny's character is fictional but her life is the story of many women who had an absent mother and were traumatized and abused as young girls. Their adult life and lifestyles continued to be marked with patterns of abuse, trauma, and exploitation.

Often adults who were abused as children lack the ability to set appropriate boundaries. This includes boundaries that keep us safe from others as well as boundaries that help us manage our own behavior.

> *"Any time I tried to say how I felt my mom got mad.*
> *I learned to keep my mouth shut and*
> *everything would be ok." Susan*

Whenever Susan tried to have an opinion or a different idea than her mom, mom would get mad and verbally berate Susan. She learned that setting boundaries conveyed her resistance or refusal to submit which only enraged her mom causing more rejection or abuse.

Not having boundaries, limits or protective resistance may appease the abuser, stall the violence, or deflect the abuser's anger, diminish the abuse, or even initiate peace.

## *Signs of weak boundaries ~*

- ❖ Being submissive
- ❖ Unable to say no
- ❖ Accepting responsibility for other people's actions and responses
- ❖ Focusing on other people
- ❖ Being over-responsible or irresponsible
- ❖ Giving away your power or taking too much power

❖ Having no sense of privacy in a relationship

❖ Invading other's rights sexually

❖ Emotionally dependent

❖ People pleasing

With very good intentions we teach our daughters (and sons) how to be safe. We talk about "stranger danger," and not to go anywhere with someone they don't know. We talk about their private parts and never allow someone to touch them or to hurt them. We teach them self-defense and empower them to say "NO!"

However, when defenses (words or actions) fail to stand up against someone in authority or anyone trusted, the feeling of shame can be intensified. If the abuser was stronger or more powerful and won against them, feelings of failure and self-contempt can emerge.

Unable to make sense of it all, a child may arrive at the conclusion; "*It must be my fault.*"

My first memory of anything sexual was at age 4 when playing "house" with the teenage son of family friends quickly escalated to sexual abuse. Even though I felt what happened was wrong, I experienced waves of sensations; shame, fear, risk, and curiosity.

This one-time incident intermixed with other experiences established patterns of seeking experiences whereby I would draw attention sexually. I felt absolutely inadequate as a young girl with no sense of identity or boundaries.

My family went camping and I soon found the affection of the camp ranger's son. On a moonlit walk we started kissing and before I could stop him, he pushed me down on the ground and tore my pants. When I screamed, he hit me in the face busting open my lip. Suddenly he ran off and I had to find my way back to the campsite alone in the dark. There was no doubt in my mind this was my fault. I flirted with him so he would like me and willingly walked into the woods with him.

When I was 25 I owned my own business and a man came in the store with a gun, robbed the cash register and raped me. I still thought it was my fault because I wore a short skirt to work that day.

*"It must be my fault"* is reinforced by ~

- ❖ Why didn't you ...
- ❖ You should have...
- ❖ You could have...
- ❖ How many times have I told you not to...
- ❖ Didn't I tell you to never to...
- ❖ How could you have...

Concerning abuse or exploitation, absolutely no form of blame, implied or imposed, should ever be placed on the victim. Implying the victim was in any way at fault instills shame and guilt and suggests the victim had control or responsibility in what happened.

Within the context of a particular incident there may be points of confusion as to who is at fault. Sorting out responsibility is a huge part of effective prayer ministry so that any unresolved internal or spiritual conflict gets dealt with.

Any belief in the lie that abuse was "my fault" can warp and twist into the belief the victim had the power to stop it or allow it to happen. If this belief isn't replaced with the truth, it partners with a form of witchcraft, believing you have the power to make someone behave or perform in a certain way.

Coming out of agreement with the lie that abuse was "my fault" and any resulting lie of "false power" is essential to getting free from this type of shame.

*Sorting it out ~*

* ❖ Determine who is responsible. What did they do, say, or imply vs. what did I do, say or imply, if anything?
* ❖ Give back responsibility where it belongs, forgive, and break soul-bonding.
* ❖ Repent for believing the lie it was your fault, ask God's forgiveness.
* ❖ Accept responsibility for your part, if any.
* ❖ Ask God to forgive you and forgive yourself.

❖ Renounce and repent for any false power and come out of agreement with any spirit of witch-craft in Jesus name.

Although I did the same thing, it wasn't until I began counseling other sexual abuse survivors that I saw the pattern of women who had been sexually abused as children and their tendency to continue being sexually active as teens and adults.

> *My brother and his friend asked me to play*
> *with them in the basement.*
> *We hid under blankets and they messed*
> *around with me. I was scared but it felt exciting.*
> *After that, I just kept doing it." Melanie*

As a child Melanie was sexually abused by her brother and one of his friends. She was uncomfortable when it first happened but later on she went along with, and even instigated, the sexual activities. She felt special to be part of her brother's life.

Melanie became sexually active as a teen, using her femininity to seduce and attract sexual activity. When Melanie acted out in sexual ways she felt

109

empowered and in charge. Through her teens and college years Melanie manipulated scenarios through seduction, flirting, teasing, and/or being willing to give sex.

Aileen Wournos' childhood was traumatic and abusive, being exiled to the woods where she had to survive on her own. Her father was a convicted child molester. By her early teens Aileen was prostituting herself for money and pregnant at 14. The first time she felt in love was with a woman. The relationship caused Aileen to try, for the first time, to stop prostitution and look for other employment. Unable to find work, she returned to prostitution for money.

Aileen began to murder her clients to get money without performing sexually. Even in court Aileen was harsh, unrepentant and believed she was a victim, merely defending herself. She was tried and convicted as a serial killer and in 2003 was the 10th woman to die by execution in the United States since 1961. Her biography is portrayed in the 2003 movie entitled, "Monster."

All abuse isn't traumatic, but all trauma is abusive. A young girl who experiences a highly-charged traumatic event may be led as an adult to recreate scenarios that duplicate the original victimization or recreate and orchestrate the original scenario now as the one in control.

Some women may reenact not only the same scenario but also the exact behavioral experience sometimes leading them to victimize in the same way they were victimized.

## *Examples of reenacting ~*

- ❖ Doing the same self-destructive behavior over and over again, usually something that took place in childhood and started with a trauma
- ❖ Reliving a "story" from the past
- ❖ Engaging in abusive relationships repeatedly
- ❖ Repeating painful experiences including specific behavior, scenes, persons and feelings
- ❖ Doing something to others that you experienced through trauma

More complicated is the area of sexual acting out that occurs in the presence of extreme danger, violence, risk or shame. Including are relationships saturated with arousal escalators -- supercharged sex, violence, dramatic exits, passionate reconciliations, secrets and threats of abandonment.

## *Examples of high arousal behaviors ~*

- ❖ Feeling sexual when frightened or when violence occurs
- ❖ Difficulty completing sustained, steady tasks
- ❖ Constant search for all-or-nothing situations
- ❖ Associating with people who are dangerous to you
- ❖ Seeking high-risk sex

Experiencing a stressful, fearful and traumatic event may produce recurring unwanted responses called post traumatic stress symptoms (Post Traumatic Stress Disorder ~ PTSD).

*Examples of common post-traumatic reactions ~*

❖ Recurrent and unwanted recollections of experiences
❖ Periods of sleeplessness
❖ Sudden "real" memories (vivid and distracting)
❖ Extremely cautious of surroundings
❖ Easily startled
❖ Distressing dreams about experiences
❖ Flashbacks as if the experience is in the present
❖ Distress when exposed to reminders of the experience like holidays, birthdays, places, symbols
❖ May include physical symptoms such as trouble breathing or cold sweats

Blocking is a way to numb, anesthetize, and escape uncomfortable feelings.

*Examples of blocking ~*

❖ Excessive alcohol consumption
❖ Use of depressant drugs or "downers"
❖ TV, reading or hobbies
❖ Compulsive eating

❖ Excessive sleeping
❖ Compulsive working, especially at unrewarding jobs
❖ Compulsive exercise
❖ Bingeing
❖ Gambling
❖ Sex or fantasy
❖ Shopping/spending money

Denying pleasure is another post-traumatic stress symptom. Behaviors are self-punishing and vary from not allowing anything fun-related to partnering with extreme deprivation.

## *Examples of self-punishment ~*

❖ Have difficulty with play
❖ Perform underachieving jobs compulsively
❖ Sabotage success opportunities
❖ Denial of basic needs, food, medical care, or heat in the home
❖ Compulsive debt as a form of impoverishment
❖ Hoard money but avoid spending on legitimate needs
❖ Periods of no interest in eating or attempt drastic diets
❖ Vomit food or use diuretics/laxatives to avoid weight gain

❖ Avoid any sexual pleasure or feel remorse over feeling sexual

Stress, anxiety, fear, etc can be too much to handle. If her capacity is overloaded or overwhelmed, a woman may find another reality to visit.

Splitting off from traumatic memories might indicate dissociative identity disorder (DID), once called multiple personality disorder (MPD).

## Examples of splitting ~

❖ Fantasizing or spacing out during movies or TV that generate intense feelings or are reminders of your own original experiences

❖ Living in a fantasy world when things get tough

❖ Feeling separate from your body in reaction to a flashback

❖ Experiencing amnesia about what you are doing or where you are

❖ Living a double life

❖ Obsessing around addictive behaviors

❖ Using psychedelic drugs to escape to another place

❖ Losing yourself in romantic fantasy

Repetitive efforts of escape to relieve anxiety or to calm the body or mind, provide the feeling of being saturated with an alternate reality. The brain adjusts to compulsive behavior to feel normal; this is the subtle transference into addiction. Addiction is compulsive dependence on a behavior or substance.

Gambling, high-risk sex, stimulant drugs and high-risk activities are examples where stimulation and pleasure compensate for pain and emptiness.

In sex the possibilities are endless, sex-offending such as voyeurism or touching in public, prostitution, anonymous sex, sadomasochism all rely on danger and/or fear to escalate arousal and sexual high.

Some relationships are inundated with arousal escalators mentioned earlier -- supercharged sex, violence, dramatic exits, passionate reconciliations, secrets and threats of abandonment, etc.

Sexual arousal accesses chemicals in the brain that are very compelling. If your brain adjusts to it, you would need the stimulation simply to feel normal.

Sex is complicated by release of a brain chemical called "dopamine" during orgasm which adds an intensely addictive component.

The combination of high escalators and the subsequent release of dopamine is a highly volatile set up for sexual addiction. Women dealing with sexual addiction have told me that post-orgasm is the only time they feel at peace.

Components of soap operas are filled with what we typically call "drama." Drama usually comes from trauma; the beginning of intense-based relationships, where intensity is substituted for intimacy.

# 9

## *Women Have Lipstick*

*"Therefore this is what the Sovereign LORD says:
'Because you people have brought to mind your
guilt by your open rebellion, revealing your sins in all
that you do—because you have done this,
you will be taken captive."
—Ezekiel 21:24*

Watching television one night I caught the middle of a movie where 1940's gangsters rob a bank and capture one of the female clerks as hostage.

Returning to their hideout, the gangsters demand the shy frightened clerk to "sit over there and be quiet."

The men pull out whiskey and glasses, make coarse jokes and fling their guns around, boasting in their acquisitions; the money and the hostage.

The movie's background music changes to sexy and sultry. The men stop all activity, turning their heads to gaze at the confident girlfriend strutting into the room. Her long legs are highlighted by the stiletto-heeled shoes and the tight (very tight) sweater and belted black skirt, slit perfectly up the side exposing her lower thigh.

"Hi boys," she mutters reaching across the table for a cigarette, her arm brushing up against one of the men.

The sexy girlfriend invites the shy fearful hostage into the bathroom to freshen up. The clerk is notably confused and stricken by the bold confidence of the sexy girlfriend.

The shy one stands back, curiously watching the girlfriend remove a tube of ruby red lipstick from her purse, tilting her chin up slightly to see her mirrored reflection more clearly.

Referring to the gangsters, the shy one asks her, "Aren't you afraid of them?"

With smooth strokes, the sexy one applies bright moist color to her heart-shaped full lips … pauses for a moment … then carefully presses her lips together as if to complete the ritual before she replies,

***"Men have their guns, but women have lipstick."***

She never looks at the shy one but slowly places the tube of lipstick back into her purse and smiles, glancing back into the mirror one more time before leaving the bathroom.

The shy one's intrigue and curiosity is mingled with fear and risk. For the first time she felt alive.

Consider the lyrics from the 1995 hit song by Bonnie Raitt, *I Can't Make You Love Me.*

*Turn down the lights, turn down the bed.*
*Turn down these voices inside my head.*
*Lay down with me, tell me no lies.*
*Just hold me close, don't patronize - don't patronize me*
*'Cause I can't make you love me if you don't.*
*You can't make your heart feel something it won't.*
*Here in the dark, in these final hours*
*I will lay down my heart and I'll feel the power.*
*But you won't, no you won't.*
*'Cause I can't make you love me, if you don't.*

*I'll close my eyes, then I won't see*
*The love you don't feel when you're holding me.*
*Morning will come and I'll do what's right.*
*Just give me till then to give up this fight.*
*And I will give up this fight.*
*'Cause I can't make you love me if you don't.*
*You can't make your heart feel something it won't.*
*Here in the dark, in these final hours*
*I will lay down my heart and I'll feel the power.*

*But you won't, no you won't.*
*'Cause I can't make you love me, if you don't.*

For the moment when she is in his arms, she has his undivided attention, being desired, kissed, held; the object of his affection. In the morning when it is all over, she'll feel lonely and used, but for right now, she has the power and she has him.

> *"Everyone thought he used me for sex. Actually it is hard to admit, but I was using him". Cynthia*

From the outside Cynthia looked like the victim of a predatory man who came in and out of her life at a whim. In actuality, it was Cynthia who felt empowered when they were together sexually. She manipulated scenarios where she would lure and seduce him, meeting in secret, feeling in control.

A woman, pressed down hard enough, held back long enough and hurt deep enough, may seek her own justice. If she doesn't find peace in the midst of her storm she may emerge from her captivity by embracing her own strength—a perfect recipe for rebellion; a perfect recipe for disaster.

Power is measured by a person's ability to control their environment and others. Within the mindset of being in control, there's simply very little room for faith; that radiant place where God is actually able to empower us.

Power that is self serving aligns us with control and control aligns us with rebellion. Rebellion not only falsely promises to give back lost power through control but also grants the freedom to use that power to get what you think you need.

Rebellion isn't just a sin, but the beginning of chaos.

When rebellion is exercised through immorality it can create a lust for power, diluting and degrading our spirituality through sexuality.

> *"I always loved the bad boys; the ones on the edge; the ones I had to work hard to keep." Morgan*

Women with histories of abuse, like Morgan, may either use sex to feel power and control, or use sex to get power and control from *someone else* they perceive as powerful.

In 1995 I was horrified to learn that convicted serial killer, Charles Manson, who became an icon for evil in the late 1960's, received the most love letters in prison. Manson formed "the family" who he manipulated into brutally killing others on his behalf.

According to a Fox News Entertainment article in 2005, other notorious killers like Richard Ramirez and John Wayne Gacy had "women falling all over them."

Scott Peterson, currently in a California prison, was convicted for murdering his wife and unborn child. He, too, receives numerous love letters from women who call him a "total babe" and receives dozens of calls, letters and even marriage proposals.

Why in the world would women be drawn to evil and narcissistic personalities? They perceive them as powerful. Being associated with powerful men, even the power of darkness, gives women the illusion they are powerful too. After all, if a powerful man pays attention to me or wants me sexually, I must be powerful.

We would typically see the lighter side of power attraction through "loving a man in uniform" such as policemen, military men, and yes, Christian ministers.

Ezekiel 23 (KJV) candidly proclaims the current condition of the Israelites symbolized by a woman, Ohalah, who having been molested as a virgin child continues in sexual immorality.

*"Neither left she her whoredoms [brought] from Egypt:
for in her youth they lay with her, and they bruised the breast
of her virginity and poured their whoredom upon her."*

*"Oholah engaged in prostitution while she was still mine;
and she lusted after her lovers,
the Assyrians—warriors clothed in blue, governors
and commanders, all of them handsome young men,
and mounted horsemen."*

Paraphrasing from Genesis, Chapter 39, Joseph had risen to a place of authority and prominence in the house of Potiphar, one of King Pharoh's important officials. Second to Potiphar, Joseph held the highest authority in the household being trusted with all Potiphar's possessions and family.

Despite Potiphar's wife living in royal elegance and splendor, she was not satisfied and Joseph became her obsession.

"Lie with me," she requested, but Joseph, a faithful man of integrity and honesty, refused her. It appears the more his nobility and quest to please God emerged, the more determined she was to have him.

When all failed, she turned against Joseph and lied against him, accusing Joseph of sexually pursuing her and Joseph was sent to prison.

Potiphar's wife, had everything she could ever want; possessions, money and status, yet she lusted after Joseph, who was merely a servant in the home.

Potiphar's wife lusted after the one thing she didn't have; Joseph's anointing.

English playwright William Congreve (1690-1729) penned the line, *"Heaven has no rage like love to hatred turned, nor hell a fury like a woman scorned."*

A profound portrait of a ruthless woman is recorded alongside the story of the beheading of John the Baptist in Mark, Chapter 6.

In the backdrop of the story is Herodias who had previously been married to Philip, but deserted him for his brother Herod (already the plot for a mini-series!). John the Baptist spoke up against their sin and Herodias was furious over John's rebuke of their unlawful and incestuous marriage.

Herodias desired John's death but Herod was reluctant, fearing the multitude, who regarded John as a prophet. As a concession to appease Herodias, Herod bound John and cast him into prison.

At Herod's birthday feast, Herodias induced her daughter Salome, approximately twelve years old and skilled in sensuous dance, to perform before Herod.

Salome charmed him so much that Herod said to the girl, "Ask me for anything you want, and I'll give it to you." And he promised her with an oath, "Whatever you ask I will give you, up to half my kingdom."

She went out and said to her mother, "What shall I ask for?"

"The head of John the Baptist," Herodias answered.

She hurried to the king with the request: "I want you to give me, right now, the head of John the Baptist on a platter."

Regretfully, Herod, having made the oath public in front of his guests, could not refuse Salome's request. John the Baptist was beheaded in prison and his head brought to Herod.

John warned Herod and Herodias of their sin, but Herodias hardened her heart to the message and rebelled against God's word to her through His prophet.

Herodias not only manipulated Herod and her daughter, but conspired to kill one of God's most just and holy men. Her life had no personal boundaries or moral integrity.

Her lifestyle contained elements of betrayal, high risk behavior, seduction, incest, mother/daughter abuse, trauma, drama, witchcraft and one more; violence.

About 15 years ago I heard a message by John White, psychiatrist and author of over 20 Christian books. He pointed to Biblical and historical trends that indicate whenever there has been an increase in sexual promiscuity there was a subsequent increase in violence.

According to scripture, when the Israelites entered Cannan they found the land to be fertile beyond their expectations. But they also encountered the pagan god Baal and goddess, Asherah, worshiped by the

Cannanites for prosperity and fertility. Asherah was Baal's mistress.

Believing the pagan gods were responsible for the rich fertile land, the Israelites began to indulge in the worship customs of the Cannanites.

Asherah is portrayed as a nude, pregnant female with exaggerated breasts she holds out, symbols of the fertility she promises. Her icon was a wooden pole or stylized tree (Judges 3:7), called Asherah poles (Deut. 7:5).

Asherah was worshipped through ritualized sex and often children were sacrificed to Baal for prosperity.

Strip clubs highlight nearly naked women dancing seductively around poles, a type of fertility dance simulating the worship of Asherah, arousing men to lust after her.

Current night club dancing trends include simulating sex acts with both women and men seductively displaying "bump and grind" routines while music lyrics shout profanity and violence.

> *"In my former life I was a dancer in a club and then worked for an escort service.*
> *In my twenties I had three abortions."* **Amelia**

I understood promiscuity leading to violence after ministering to so many women post-abortion like Amelia.

Not all, but most unwanted pregnancies are symptoms of something else: immorality. And immorality increases violence; the shedding of innocent blood through abortion.

Margaret Mead, an Anglican Christian (1901-1978) was awarded the Presidential Medal of Freedom from President Jimmy Carter two years after her death. Margaret dedicated her life ambition to the study of anthropology and is a highly recognized educational contributor on the subject. Her accomplishments include teaching at Columbia and Yale universities and she founded the anthropology department at New York University. She was an author and premier contributor to the study of cultures. Margaret penned the following observation:

> *"When women venture from their traditional roles,*
> *they become more ruthless and savage than men."*

Alongside the sexual explosion among teen girls is the emergence of teen girl bullying. I just received an invitation to the 5th National Conference on *Girl Bullying and Other Forms of Relational Aggression* featuring over 1,000 professionals focused on eliminating bullying and preventing the consequences. One of the featured workshop topics is *Girls, Women, and Leadership; Teaching the Right Uses of Power*.

Being "bad" or mean is popular. The new "femme" is bold, seductive, and aggressive with big lips and huge breasts to prove it.

As a young girl I wanted larger breasts too, simply because, well, I didn't have any! Creativity serves many purposes and I invented a way, at least for a day, to have them.

At the swim center I padded my swimsuit top (by the way, they were my mom's pads … interesting!) anyway, I padded my swimsuit top so my breast looked large, much too large for a thin scrawny 11-year-old. Plunging into the water, my chest pads were forced toward the surface. Inconspicuously, I tried to squeeze out the air so they would agree to stay in the water with me.

Climbing the pool ladder to get out of the pool, the waterlogged pads began to slip down well below my breast line toward my waist. There was no choice. Holding the sagging, huge waterlogged pads tightly to my chest, I pushed off back into the water, submerging my chest below the waterline. With both hands I squeezed each pad to express the water, not realizing this would release a continuous array of beautiful tiny bubbles around me as the air expelled and water quickly filled back in. On the way home one of the water-logged pads fell out of my bag and someone ran up behind me, "is this yours?"

I have noticed women do seem obsessed with their breasts! In one day I talked with two women. One was reducing the size and the other was increasing the size!

The most preferred type of breast implant surgery is an incision around the nipple often cutting nerves. Breast implants usually cause a decrease in milk production, decreased sensitivity and often pain, rendering breast feeding nearly impossible.

The female hormone oxytocin is produced during labor and breast feeding, increasing bonding between mother and baby, initiating affection and building connection. The same hormone is secreted during sexual arousal to promote bonding in sexual partners. You can see how this is a blessing in a Godly husband and wife relationship and why casual sex was not part of God's plan.

> *"I never felt safe as a woman and always carried some type of weapon with me.*
> *I wore heavy jackets and men's clothing to appear larger than I was." Gayle*

Gayle watched her mom endure abuse and on several occasions was molested by her mom's boyfriends. She said she tried to protect herself by "acting like a boy." Being smaller in size, she wore large fitting men's clothing to feel less vulnerable. Gayle entered the military at age 23 and that is when she first began to be attracted to women.

Gayle knew clearly that God disapproved of homosexuality, but she said she could never be with a man.

*Women who deny or reject their femininity may ~*

- ❖ Believe femininity is weak
- ❖ Believe femininity is restrictive
- ❖ Believe masculinity is more powerful
- ❖ Become what their mom/dad wanted; a boy
- ❖ Become what their dad valued; strength
- ❖ Become what their mothers loved; a man
- ❖ Become what they believe is favored
- ❖ Believe another woman makes them whole
- ❖ Be with another woman for love, nurture and comfort

As women strive to become stronger emotionally and physically they also become more confident, bold, assertive, competitive, and take greater risks which is a good thing unless taken to the extreme.

You may already know that women have both estrogen (female) and testosterone (male) hormones.

Women who are unhappy with their feminine identity are sometimes encouraged to take hormone therapy that increases testosterone.

Maggie Fitzgerald (played by Hillary Swank in Clint Eastwood's 2004 Academy Award winning film, Million Dollar Baby) is a 32-year old waitress who is desperately trying to be "someone" in the competitive arena of boxing. Gym handyman, Eddie (played by Morgan Freeman), watches Maggie spend her birthday exhausting herself punching the bag and says…

> *"She came from South Western Missouri, the hills*
> *outside the town of Fiducia, set in the scene of Oak trees*
> *somewhere between no where and good by.*
> *She grew up knowing one thing; she was trash.*
> *She'd come 1800 miles*
> *but Fiducia was just over the hill."*

High levels of testosterone in women may increase aggression and sex drive but is also one of the causes of depression in women.

The extreme of anti-feminine and anti-woman are statistics that reveal annually, in the United States alone, over 38,000 women successfully trans-gender into men, surgically removing their breasts and enduring genital reconstruction. None of the documentaries or statistics I read indicate that trans-gendered women, as a whole, are more satisfied or at peace. Many continue in destructive and violent relationships.

The Sozo team, our international inner healing and deliverance ministry (www.bethelsozo.com) founded by Dawna DeSilva and Teresa Liebscher, Bethel Church, Redding, California, where I serve on staff, was hosting a training event and concluded with an invitation for prayer ministry and healing.

A person came forward who looked, dressed, talked and acted like a man. Underneath the persona was a female who already had completed partial gender reassignment, having had a double mastectomy. She was distraught and confused. She wanted to become a Christian and give her heart to Christ. Confessing what she had done, she then asked the team, "What do I do now? Am I a boy or a girl?"

> *"After I got married, all the sex stopped and I began to gain weight. I just didn't want him to touch me."*
> **Susanna**

Before she married, Susanna felt sexy and empowered when her fiancé desired her. She drew him in and he was smitten over her, doing whatever it took to make her happy. Within months after getting married, Susanna changed. She no longer felt sexy and had gained almost 30 lbs. She felt cheap and ashamed, hiding her body while undressing and feeling uncomfortable when her husband approached her sexually.

Living within our own ideal and strength may work for a season but soon we learn in relationship to God and others, it is inadequate at best. It is the fear of pain that drives us away from finding true intimacy. We can become afraid of love and settle for so much less.

The price women have paid attempting to find freedom has brought even greater captivity. All that "freedom" isn't so free.

Women who desire to be like men set their standards too low. I believe within the broad scope of feminism is the idolatry of females who replicate themselves in the image of a man. Why do we need to artificially hyper inflate our breasts, ride the power of someone else, or protest for equal rights to men?

When we are created in the image of a great and mighty God, why would we settle for the image of a man? Men don't hold the key to our freedom, Jesus does.

In our youth we were covered by grace. As adult women choosing our own justice and covering, we forfeited that grace by resuming the practices of our youth, from the years of captivity "while in Egypt."

When we alienate from God and trust in our own strength those practices will flip and in turn become our punishment. The enemy will double back and retaliate using the object of our trust as our punishment to shame us. Not because God ordered the punishment, rather our own behavior alienated us from true love, intimacy, and relationship with God.

Rebellion doesn't win; it doesn't bring justice; it doesn't bring peace. Greater are the consequences of rebellion than of its causes.

Trusting in our own strength or the strength of anyone other than God is rebellion manifested through both adultery and idolatry.

## Idolatry ~

❖ Using all our gifts and strength to serve our self
  - Conforming our self into another's image
  - Conforming our self into our own image

The consequences of our attempts to protect, save and redeem ourself is made clear in the light of His presence; the feeling of shame and separation. In other words, when we rebel and walk in an anti-Christ spirit, we, by default, choose punishment and alienation over love.

## Coming home ~

❖ Recognize you are not that powerful!

❖ Renounce false power

❖ Ask God to forgive you

- for rebellion
- for seeking your own justice
- for not trusting Him
- for seeking ungodly places of refuge
- for idolatry

❖ Forgive yourself

❖ Break ungodly and unholy soul ties

❖ Ask the Holy Spirit to fill you

It takes compassion and empathy to minister to broken women. We need the patience and commitment to walk alongside them *through* the pain into freedom.

When we look at the overall condition of women in the world, we see how much *we* need the transforming power of God to extend grace and pour out love.

His love, which is pure, will, like water, seep in and repair the great breaches within the heart of women.

We cannot do it without His eyes, arms and most of all His love.

Today you can return to love and the One who knows you best and loves you the most.

His heart for us...

*I made you grow like a plant of the field.*
*You grew up and developed and became the*
*most beautiful of jewels. Your breasts were formed and your*
*hair grew, you who were naked and bare.*

*Later I passed by, and when I looked at you and saw that you were old enough for love, I spread the corner of my garment over you and covered your nakedness.*

*I gave you my solemn oath and entered into a covenant with you, declares the Sovereign LORD, and you became mine.*

*I bathed you with water and washed the blood from you and put ointments on you.*

*I clothed you with an embroidered dress and put leather sandals on you. I dressed you in fine linen and covered you with costly garments.*

*I adorned you with jewelry: I put bracelets on your arms and a necklace around your neck, and I put a ring on your nose, earrings on your ears and a beautiful crown on your head.*

*So you were adorned with gold and silver; your clothes were of fine linen and costly fabric and embroidered cloth. Your food was fine flour, honey and olive oil. You became very beautiful and rose to be a queen.*

*And your fame spread among the nations on account of your beauty, because the splendor I had given you made your beauty perfect, declares the Sovereign LORD.*

Ezekiel 16:7-14

# 10

## A Date With Justice

> *"Then I heard a loud voice in heaven say: Now have come the salvation and the power and the kingdom of our God, and the authority of his Christ. For the accuser of our brothers, who accuses them before our God day and night, has been hurled down."*
>
> —Rev 12:10

Principles that hold higher value than relationship create form without purpose and tradition without power.   Living in our own strength produces religious activity, forming our identity to a principle rather than a relationship. When religion is fueled by shame or fear it will attempt to find God through performance and works, following rules and regulations, rather than through love and grace.

The truth that sets you free will never be found through mental gymnastics or religious principles. Instead the truth is found in journey outside of our self into a journey of discovering Him.

Intimacy is both the ability and the choice to be close, loving and vulnerable. Intimacy requires identity development. You have to know and trust yourself in order to share your self with another. Knowing yourself makes it possible to join with honesty and confidence in intimate relationship without using manipulation, fear, or control.

God describes love in great detail in the Bible, especially in 1 Corinthians, chapter 13.

Let's take God's love and apply it to a human relationship.

*What if a person who loved you~*

- ❖ Responds with patience, kindness, and is not envious of you?

- ❖ Is not boastful or prideful?

- ❖ Is not rude toward you or self-seeking or easily angered?

- ❖ Does not keep any record of your wrongs?

❖ Refuses to be deceitful and is always truthful with you?

❖ Protects you, trusts you, always hopes for your good, and perseveres through conflicts with you?

❖ Does not want you for sex and treasures every moment you spent with them?

❖ Makes plans with you for your future and desires you to prosper in all you do?

❖ Provides unlimited creativity and wisdom?

❖ Can understand and know what you need, answering and responding before you can ask?

❖ Gives you a full partnership, power and authority to rule in the kingdom they own?

This is how God defines the type of love and intimate connection He wants us to experience. He describes love that is giving, rather than self-seeking. And there's the problem. What human can live up to this?

Most women have never felt pursued, loved and adored for who they are. They never felt claimed or ac-knowledged. They have never felt they are worthy of someone sacrificing their life so they could live free.

In both the Old and New Testament, God used farming principles as examples. Those analogies relate to farming the soil of the ground as well as farming the soil of our heart.

For example:

"*Do not plant two kinds of seed in your vineyard; if you do, not only the crops you plant but also the fruit of the vineyard will be defiled.*" Deut. 22:9.

"*Jesus told them another parable: "The kingdom of heaven is like a man who sowed good seed in his field."* Matthew 13:24

"*For you know that it was not with perishable things such as silver or gold that you were redeemed from the empty way of life handed down to you from your forefathers, but with the precious blood of Christ, a lamb without blemish or defect.*

*He was chosen before the creation of the world, but was revealed in these last times for your sake.*

*Through him you believe in God, who raised him from the dead and glorified him, and so your faith and hope are in God.*

*Now that you have purified yourselves by obeying the truth so that you have sincere love for your brothers, love one another deeply, from the heart.*

*For you have been born again, not of perishable seed, but of imperishable, through the living and enduring word of God.*" 1Peter 1:17-23

The KJV of the Bible states 1Peter 1:18 in a way more clear for my point. "*Forasmuch as ye know that ye were not redeemed with corruptible things, [as] silver and* gold, from your vain conversation [received] by tradition from your fathers."

And 1Peter 1:23 like this... "*Being born again, not of corruptible seed, but of incorruptible by the word of God, which liveth and abideth for ever.*"

When God planted the seed of life in Mary it was an incorruptible seed. "*The angel answered, The Holy Spirit will come upon you, and the power of the Most High will overshadow you. So the holy one to be born will be called the Son of God,*" (Luke 1:35).

Mary had never received the seed of a man, she was a pure virgin. Her purity was fertile ground for the Most High to overshadow her and fill her with His presence.

Society has taken what God has said about love and intimacy and changed it into emotions and feelings that sexualize and poorly imitate genuine love. Young girls and women tell me story after story of receiving counterfeit love and yet, they are desperate for another man to fill their life. The anti-Christ spirit offers a substitute; a counterfeit. That is, false love through sexual encounters. The enemy loves to play women in this area because he knows it hurts the heart of God.

However, as long as women bow to a substitute in place of a genuine spiritual relationship with Jesus they will remain infertile spiritually.

Internet pornography is sweeping through homes and through the hearts of men and women at a rapid pace planting seeds of destruction and contaminating the marriage beds of their future.

We have moved so far from a God centered union that men visit sperm banks, make a deposit, and a woman can make withdrawals without ever seeing or knowing the man whose seed she has received.

The woman at the well was married 5 times. All her life she lived lower than her calling. She settled for the seed of a man until Jesus offered her the real deal. *"...whoever drinks the water I give him will never thirst. Indeed, the water I give him will become in him a spring of water welling up to eternal life." (John 4:14)*

Jesus, alone is the resurrection and the life (John 11:25). He covers our nakedness and clothes us with dignity and purity. God wants you to arise beyond yourself and your unclean past.

Healing within the sexual relationship of a marriage is possible when both partners are willing to stay present with each other, pray together and allow vulnerability. God doesn't want to restore broken relationships, He wants to rebuild them.

We are called (1Peter 1:16:17) to be holy, set apart for Him.

*"But just as he who called you is holy, so be holy in all you do; for it is written: "Be holy, because I am holy."*

We cannot make ourselves holy and pure. It requires receiving the incorruptible Jesus and thereby, receiving God's love, grace, mercy, and forgiveness.

God, who knows you and everything about you, loves you perfectly.

Surrender requires being real. Oswald Chambers says in *My Utmost for His Highest* says to every degree in which we are not real; we will dispute rather than come to Jesus. When someone runs to anything or anyone but Jesus, their action indicates they don't trust Him. And if they aren't trusting in Him, they are trusting in something else.

Surrender is an opportunity to deal with pain in a different way. Rather than looking for an escape it requires actually holding onto the pain long enough to take it to Jesus and allow Him to lead us out.

Loss positions you for justice and transparency unleashes breakthrough. The perils and tribulations of living in a fallen world give us an opportunity to press into His presence.

When we surrender to God's grace we are laid bare by the light of His presence.

## In His Presence ~

- ❖ In the presence of His integrity, our own pretense is exposed.

- ❖ In the presence of His constancy, our cowardice is brought to light.

- ❖ In the presence of His fierce love for us, our own nakedness and hardness of heart is revealed.

143

❖ In His presence, there is nothing left to earn; nothing left to prove; nothing left to lose.

Forgiveness is a fruit of surrender. Those who surrender their lives to God choose to forgive, not because they should, but because they want to. Forgiveness is the courage to let mercy triumph over judgment (James 2:13).

God provided forgiveness for people who were destined to fail but who chose to return to God. In the Old Testament, sin was forgiven through sacrificial offerings. Then God sent his son, Jesus, who for all time *is* the sacrifice for sin. It is through Jesus we have forgiveness, and because we have been forgiven we can forgive others.

In forgiving, we release our judgment or desire for revenge. The forgiver pays a great price and the guilty go free. This is the example that Christ gave us. He forgave and we go free.

Unforgiveness will never remedy a wrong or fix the problem. Wrong doing, even when forgiven, may have perpetuated consequences that we no longer have the power to control or change. In most cases the damage is either irreparable or irreplaceable.

Anger, shame, fear and rebellion are ways to control and find our own remedy and justice. Not anyone who hurt you can give you back what was stolen or give you adequate justice. No matter how much you hurt yourself, blame yourself, or punish yourself, it will not bring justice.

We forgive because repair and repayment is impossible and unforgiveness is a death-grip on pain; a deep pain that creates strongholds that fight against the power and presence of God.

Jesus is our date with justice. Jesus was God's sacrifice to redeem us, reveal His love, and give us a future. Jesus brings justice through His atonement. There is a cleansing (1 John 1:9) and healing (Ps. 103:3 and Ps. 147:3) element associated with Jesus sacrifice; God's restitution. The purity of Jesus' shed Blood washes us, not just covering over, but removing any stain or odor, any residue or evidence. Receiving forgiveness is partnering with God's love and accepting incorruptible Jesus.

Resistance to love and intimate connection is fortified by promises we made to protect ourselves. We can no longer afford to keep these promises. Jesus wants our stability, security, and significance to be in Him. To live in your true identity in full intimacy with Him we must risk believing what He offers is more important and more worthy than what we can do for our self.

Jesus suffered and paid the price for our purity, healing and freedom. Jesus was the remedy for God's wrath and the substitute for God's punishment. Jesus took our suffering upon Himself. Jesus died so we could live emotionally, physically, spiritually, and eternally free with full access to the benefits of a good, loving God. Because of Jesus, we are unpunishable.

We were called unto Him and claimed from the beginning and God never renounced his right over us. In the Old Testament, when His people strayed away and worshipped other gods and had other lovers, God sent His Prophets to call, draw, and persuade our return, announcing His love for us.

In the New Testament, He pursued us by sending Himself, in the person of Jesus, to bring justice and freedom; to bring us back to His heart.

Jesus releases us from slavery and places us in the Glory of His dominion, His Kingdom…on earth as it is in Heaven!

Surrender is a release of control and repentance puts us back to the highest place with God. It is returning to the "pent" house of God; returning to your seat (Ephesians 2:6) in the Heavens, reserved for you since the beginning of time.

Jesus fulfills the desire of a woman's longing. It isn't doing something for Him. It is *being* with Him without barriers.

> *"And we, who with unveiled faces all reflect the Lord's glory, are being transformed into his likeness with ever-increasing glory, which comes from the Lord, who is the Spirit."*
> *2 Cor. 3:18*

It is our "unveiled face" that reflects His glory and everything is to lead us into His embrace—the resting place of His Presence.

## Now *is the time* ~

- ❖ It is time we stop punishing ourselves and withholding love due to shame, fear or rebellion.

- ❖ It is time to stop performance and self centered strength.

- ❖ It is time we put aside religious traditions and works.

- ❖ It is time we stop looking for an ordinary man to set us free.

- ❖ It is time to take down the high places that have been exalted above the knowledge of God.

- ❖ It is time to come alive and stop receiving corruptible substitutes.

*Listen! My lover! Look! Here he comes, leaping across the mountains, bounding over the hills.*

*My lover is like a gazelle or a young stag. Look! There he stands behind our wall, gazing through the windows, peering through the lattice.*

*My lover spoke and said to me, "Arise, my darling, my beautiful one, and come with me.*

*See! The winter is past; the rains are over and gone.*
*Flowers appear on the earth; the season of singing has come,*
*the cooing of doves is heard in our land.*
*Songs 2:8-11*

The one who comes to her Lover is the one who no longer wants to cling to worthless idols or forfeit the grace that He gives. (Jonah 2:8)

The one who comes to Him is rescued from the dominion of darkness and brought into His Kingdom of light (Col. 1:13).

The one who comes to her beloved has demolished arguments and every pretension that has set itself up against the knowledge of God and takes every thought captive in obedience to Jesus (2 Cor. 10:5).

His invitation arrived and it's up to you.

## Accepting your date with justice ~

❖ Fall into the arms of Jesus.

❖ Confess manipulation, rebellion, self-punishing, control, and fear.

❖ Confess allowing an unclean spirit as a substitute for love.

❖ Confess the vows and promises you can no longer afford to keep.

- ❖ Confess the high places you allowed to be exalted against the knowledge and power of God.

- ❖ Receive Jesus forgiveness.

- ❖ Give forgiveness to others who hurt you.

- ❖ Give forgiveness to yourself, which is often the hardest, but absolutely necessary.

- ❖ Release all offenses and judgments against others and your self.

- ❖ Remain in His arms; remain in His presence.


Who is this?  She is the one who comes out of the wilderness leaning on her Lover (Songs 8:5). She has surrendered to Him and now they are one.

There is no one left to blame you, shame you, condemn you, judge you, hate you, hold you back, keep you down or stop you.

*"For the accuser of our brothers, who accuses them before our God day and night, has been hurled down."*
*Rev 12:10*


**Who are your accusers now?**

# 11

## One Size Fits All

*"I will extend peace to her like a river, and the wealth of nations like a flooding stream; you will nurse and be carried on her arm and dandled on her knees."*

*— Isaiah 66:12*

Have you ever gone shopping and found a top you like? Then you look at the tag and it says "one size fits all." Most adult women know this is a lie but we still try it on just to prove we were right. If I try it on and it doesn't fit, I change the tag to "one size fits some."

151

I tried on a top with a tag, "slightly irregular." Now, honestly, how irregular could "slightly" be? Looking in the mirror, one sleeve was below my hand and the other above my elbow. That was a little more than slightly, don't you think? And finally I learned Victoria's Secret; that no one over a size 10 can find anything in the store to fit properly.

I think this could be reflective of women. We are certainly not all one size, sometimes slightly irregular, and very few of us are a perfect 10.

Swiss theologian and priest, Hans Urs von Balthasar (1905-1968) pointed out that all of human civilization depends on love at first sight, namely, that women, when presented with their newborn babies for the first time, will fall in love with them. Why they do this is difficult to understand. After all, this is not a good time for meeting new people and making new friends. Hans confesses he has no experience of the process, but witnessed it a number of times, and it seemed to him that women are not at their best at these moments. In fact, they seem to be downright cranky!

God's pure love does not compare with earth's best parents and does not fluctuate from delight to cranky. God's love is complete and represents the perfect love of two parents, mother and father.

Although neither male nor female, God creates us male and female in His image, which contains the attributes of both genders (Genesis 1:27).

What ever our gender is, it can reflect that particular nature and image of God. He is the true "one size fits all," always regular, and a perfect 10!

Being created in His image as a female makes us aware He knows us, how we feel, and what we need.

If we only look to God in the image of a father, we can be swayed to believe He is not able to comfort the unmet needs of women or to provide maternal love in the absence of a mother. We need to know God understands what it is like to suffer menstrual cramps or the loss of a breast from cancer.

It is important for us, as women, to embrace His full revelation to us, which includes what we might label as feminine characteristics.

The Interpreter's Bible Dictionary sees it highly significant that the Hebrew term for the uniquely female organ, the uterus (womb), is used in the original Scriptures to describe God's compassion.

One of God's Hebrew names is El-Shaddai which means *God Almighty*. *El* points to the power of God, Himself. *Shaddai* seems to be derived from another word meaning *breast*, which implies that Shaddai signifies one who nourishes, supplies, and satisfies.

It is God as *El* who helps, but it is God as *Shaddai* who abundantly blesses with all manner of blessings. God has complete sufficiency to nourish His women into fruitfulness.

God desires to bless women and provide in abundance all of her needs. El Shaddai is indicative of a God who is powerful enough to do just that.

Who can forget Big Mama Papa in William Young's 2007 book, The Shack? *"Mackenzie, I am neither male nor female, even though both genders are derived from my nature. If I choose to appear to you as a man or a woman, it is because I love you."*

The Shekinah Glory of God literally means *"to dwell, or to live with."* As an interesting note I learned that "Shekinah" in Hebrew is actually a feminine noun.

John 14:16 introduces the nurturing Presence of the Holy Spirit as a counselor, *"And I will ask the Father, and he will give you another Counselor to be with you forever."* And in John 14:26 (KJV) as a comforter, *"But the Comforter [which is] the Holy Ghost, whom the Father will send in my name, he shall teach you all thing and bring all things to your remembrance..."*

Attributes of counsel, comfort, and teaching are tender characteristics of the Holy Spirit. Matthew 3:16 refers to the Holy Spirit as a gentile dove descending upon Jesus.

All feminine traits considered, He has chosen in scripture to be called God and by male pronouns without any further need of explanation to us, so I respectfully honor God in His chosen title.

However, we can love and apprehend God's tender or maternal traits without being dishonoring or demeaning, looking to God to satisfy our unmet need for a mother's love.

*A mother's blessing ~*

*I have examined your heart and know*
*everything about you.*
*I know when you sit down or stand up.*
*I know your every thought even when you feel far away.*
*I chart the path ahead of you and tell you where to stop*
*and rest.*
*Every moment I know where you are.*
*I know what you will say even before you say it.*
*I both proceed and follow you.*
*I place my hand of blessing on your head.*
*Such knowledge is great.*
*You can never be taken away from my Spirit.*
*My Presence is always with you.*
*If you go to up to visit heaven, I am there.*
*If you ride the wings of the morning,*
*I will dwell there by the oceans.*
*My hand will guide you and my strength*
*will support you.*
*You could ask the darkness to hide you*
*and the light around you to become night,*
*but even in the darkness I am with you.*

*I made all the delicate inner parts of your body*
*and knit you together in my womb.*
*I have made you so wonderfully and*
*my workmanship is marvelous – you know it is true.*
*I watched you being formed in seclusion,*
*woven together in my secret place.*
*I saw you before you were born.*
*Every day of your life is recorded in my book.*
*Every moment was laid out before a*
*single day had passed.*
*All my thoughts toward you are precious;*
*they cannot be counted and outnumber*
*the grains of sand.*
*When you awake in the morning*
*I am there with you.*
*(Adapted from Psalm 139: 1-18)*


*"Can a mother forget the baby at her breast and*
*have no compassion on the child she has borne?*
*Though she may forget, I will not forget you!"*
*Isaiah 49:15*

*"As a mother comforts her child, so I will comfort*
*you…" Isaiah 66:13*

*"I pray also that the eyes of your heart may be
enlightened in order that you may know
the hope to which he has called you,
the riches of his glorious inheritance in the saints,
and his incomparably great power for us who believe.*

*That power is like the working of his mighty strength,
which he exerted in Christ when
he raised him from the dead and seated him
at his right hand in the heavenly realms, far above all
rule and authority, power and dominion,
and every title that can be given,
not only in the present age but also in the one to come."*
*Eph 1:18-21*

HOPE IS the ability to hear the music of the future.

FAITH IS the courage to dance to it in the present.

LOVE IS the act of asking someone else to dance
with you.

# 12

## Crowns & Swords

*"Let us rejoice and be glad and give him glory!*
*For the wedding of the Lamb has come,*
*and his bride has made herself ready."*

**—Revelation 19:7**

Women are a lot like cats. They love to have their backs rubbed but look out if you touch the wrong spot! Those claws can pop out like switch blades and before you can say, "I am sorry," the damage has been done.

Much of our relationship with other women centers around jealousy, competition, and fear. When we move into competition and self-protection, pushing other women away, we behave like the hurtful mothers we grew up with. When we hurt other women, we hurt our-self and our own gender suffers separation and loss.

To become the role models for the next generation means we must begin to heal and bridge the gaps in female relationships. We have to begin to heal within our gender, one woman and one daughter at a time.

This is absolutely essential for women to fulfill their role as spiritual mothers. We have to love and care for other women as God loves us.

## *Building bridges ~*

- ❖ Ask God to forgive you for being jealous or competitive toward other women.

- ❖ Ask God to forgive you for being selfish or controlling.

- ❖ Ask God to help you love unconditional.

- ❖ Ask God to fill you with compassion and understanding.

- ❖ Ask God to bring you a spiritual mother to walk along side you.

- ❖ Ask God to bring you a spiritual daughter to mentor.

Fulfilled Girl – Receives her authentic identity

Fulfilled Daughter – Receives her full inheritance

Fulfilled Wife – Embraces and offers genuine intimacy

Fulfilled Mother – Empowers out of love

He says, "…but wait, there is still more…"

God has not kept His mysteries a secret. He has not hid them from us but rather He has hid them *for* us (Proverbs 25:2). Jesus' ministry was a model; a live teaching demonstration.

Jesus held all power from His Father. The disciples operated in healing and deliverance under the umbrella of Jesus so they would experience His corporate anointing.

Jesus showed how to partner with our Heavenly Father through performing miracles, healing the sick, raising the dead, casting out demons, and cleansing the leper (Matt: 10: 7,8).

Then Jesus made a profound statement that commissioned us to do the same. He went further by telling us that we would do even **greater** things. *"I tell you the truth, anyone who has faith in me will do what I have been doing. He will do even greater things than these, because I am going to the Father"* (John 14:12).

The disciples functioned under Jesus' anointing but later had to operate under their personal anointing through the Holy Spirit (Acts 1:7). Our power comes from the corporate anointed atmosphere of the Presence of God. Our authority comes from what Jesus is doing in us.

When Father God resurrected Jesus from the dead and went to His Father, we were given power and authority and released into the realm of the impossible. We come into agreement with power and authority by stewarding both the Presence of God and who Jesus is in us; the resurrection and the life.

Jesus was anointed (smeared) with the Holy Spirit. Our power comes from being smeared with a personal experience from the Holy Spirit. The disciples waited (Acts 2:8) for the anointing to come.

"Yippie, skippie," all that healing and God's love, anointing and provision is wonderful...and let us not leave home without it!

If you have any illness or pain in your body, let's approach Heaven right now and partner with Him in healing.

*Healing your body ~*

❖ Forgive anyone who hurt you.

❖ Ask God to forgive you for any abuse to your body due to self-punishment.

- ❖ Accept God's love.

- ❖ Ask God to forgive you for any way you have been angry or hateful toward your body.

- ❖ Put your hand on your chest and ask your body to forgive you for any way you abused yourself through stress, addictions, over-work, or …

- ❖ Name any illness or sickness and command it to go.

- ❖ Command any pain to go.

- ❖ Command your body, muscles, and tissues to release any lingering affects of trauma from abuse or accidents.

- ❖ Ask God to release peace to your mind and body.

- ❖ To activate your prayers, try to do something you couldn't do before you prayed.

- ❖ Thank Him for improvement and press in for more!

## *A story: Crowns and Swords ~*

The Princess was crowned the day she was born. She grew and learned to be a daughter while living in the house of her father, a King.

Her identity was formed in relationship to the One who loved her unconditionally. He gave her a sword that was just her size and she watched and copied everything the King did.

If she fell or got hurt, He picked her up and healed all her pain. She learned to rest in His arms, trusting His guidance and love.

He watched her proudly as her femininity developed like a delicate budding blossom, pure and fragrant. It was good. He smiled at her often as she twirled and danced around the room holding her sword high over her head.

When her capacity for intimacy was expanded and her heart longed for greater love, another crown was prepared for her and she made herself ready.

The King called her into His Presence and she beheld the Glory of her King. He brought forth a new bigger sword and bestowed it to her.

The sword was heavy so she held it with both hands, wielding it uncontrollably when a shout came forth from her innermost being, "no more...no more." The sword fell to the ground; too heavy to lift and soon out of reach.

The dark was too dark; the silence too quiet. Time passed she gave in to unbelief, doubt and disappointment.

She saw the sword a far distance away. It was motionless and dull, so she asked, "Was it destined for another?"

The King never left her side. He stayed with her through her darkest moment until the unloving in her cried to be loved and His Presence so great she had to choose.

She collapsed at His feet, weeping and forgiving. She repented for her fears and laid down her offenses, religious performance and self-protection until there was nothing left to give up.

He covered her with a fresh new garment of His love and placed the sword in her hand once again. In her grasp, the sword came alive. She held it over her head and the first sweep was to cut the chains around her ankles. She cried aloud for enough strength and His love strengthened her.

The sword moved swift and mighty; the chains broke and shame was gone.

He washed her with the Blood of the Lamb and He placed a flowing mantle of glistening white light over her shoulders. He brought forth the jeweled crown of a Queen, anointed with oil, and placed it on her head.

He kissed her forehead and invited her to sit at His side. He whispered in her ear secrets of His Kingdom. He looked into her eyes and imparted a vision for her sisters, those not yet mature.

Her heart expanded and her breasts became like towers, filled with the mother's heart of God.

### And now, my fair one, my sister,
### I pass the sword to you...

*"We have a young sister, and her breasts are not yet grown.*
*What shall we do for our sister for the day she is spoken for?*
*If she is a wall, we will build towers of silver on her.*
*If she is a door, we will enclose her with panels of cedar.*
*Beloved, I am a wall, and my breasts are like towers.*
*Thus I have become in his eyes like one bringing contentment."*
*Songs 8:8-10*

### Will you accept the challenge?

### Will you allow yourself to be captivated by Him?

### Will you risk moving closer?

### Will you love?

### Will you trust Him to remove all the shame?

### Will you carry the mothering heart of God?

### Will you empower the next generation of daughters?

### Will you?

*Your assignment, should you choose to accept it ~*

❖ Demonstrate the will of God, here and now, through His radical Presence and power.

❖ Answer women's hearts by prophesying their destiny.

166

There is nothing more powerful than a woman who is fully breasted, fully clothed and in her right mind (the mind of Christ)!

The only thing you might add is a microphone! Say it loud; say it like you mean it; say it with me,

**"*I am a Woman made in God's image...*"**

*I* am a *Woman*

made in GOD'S image

**accepted   adopted**

**redeemed**

*enlightened  endowed  blessed*

**set free   set apart   loved**

*holy  healed  delivered*

*refined   renewed   equipped*

**covered   complete   blameless**

**unashamed   unafraid**

**forgiven**

*H*is chosen

*H*is friend

*H*is bride

*I* am a *Woman*

made in GOD'S image

*destined for such a time as this* ~

If you have a testimony you would like to share as a result of reading this book, Yvonne would love to hear from you.

# Additional Ministry

## Host or attend a workshop

### I am a Woman ~ Healing the Feminine Spirit

### Dancing on the Grave of Your Past

❖ Book

❖ Experience the healing journey companion workbook

❖ Support Group Facilitator's Guide

### Prophetic Gates – Partnering with Creative Expression

More information at

www.StillwaterLavender.com

# About the Author

With 25 years experience in prophetic pastoring, emotional healing and trauma resolution, Yvonne serves on Pastoral Counseling staff in the Transformation Center at Bethel Church in Redding, CA. as part of their counseling and Bethel Sozo team.

Yvonne is an author, conference speaker, third-year Bethel School of Supernatural Ministry graduate, and hosts articles and Q/A column for the Christian Quarterly entitled *Talk With Yvonne.*

As an ordained minister, Yvonne's passion is to see people acquire their Kingdom identity, inheritance, intimacy and authority. She is available for speaking or personal ministry.

Yvonne is the author of:

*I am a Woman ~ Healing the Feminine Spirit*

*Dancing on the Graves of Your Past series:*

*Book, workbook and group leader's guide*

*Prophetic Gates ~ Partner with creative expression*

*Prayers of Prophetic Declaration*

*Prophetic Declarations for Teens*

## Contact Information

### Yvonne Martinez

(530) 229-7909 x 3040

yvonnem@ibethel.org

or

talkwithyvonne@hotmail.com


Transformation Center / Bethel Church

933 College View

Redding, CA 96003


Bethel Sozo information  www.bethelsozo.com

Bethel Church information  www.ibethel.org


Books available at

www.StillwaterLavender.com

Made in the USA
San Bernardino, CA
13 October 2015